Multicultural Partnerships

Involve All Families

Darcy J. Hutchins

Marsha D. Greenfeld

Joyce L. Epstein

Mavis G. Sanders

Claudia L. Galindo

Routledge
Taylor & Francis Group
New York London

First published 2012 by Eye On Education

Published 2013 by Routledge
711 Third Avenue, New York, NY 10017, USA
2 Park Square, Milton Park, Abingdon, Oxon OX14 4RN

Routledge is an imprint of the Taylor & Francis Group, an informa business

Library of Congress Cataloging-in-Publication Data

Hutchins, Darcy J.
Multicultural partnerships : involve all families / Darcy J. Hutchins, Marsha D. Greenfeld, Joyce L. Epstein, Mavis G. Sanders, and Claudia L. Galindo.
    pages cm
Includes bibliographical references.
ISBN 978-1-59667-210-9
1. Multicultural education--United States.
2. Multicultural education--Activity programs--United States.
3. Education--Parent participation--United States.
I. Title.
LC1099.3.H88 2012
370.1170973--dc23   2011044668

Cover Designer: Jennifer Osterhouse Graphic Design
Illustrator: Paul Kirchner
ISBN: 978-1-596-67210-9 (pbk)

Also Available from Eye On Education

Family Reading Night
Darcy J. Hutchins, Marsha D. Greenfeld, & Joyce L. Epstein

Teach My Kid—I Dare You!
The Educator's Essential Guide to Parent Involvement
Sherrel Bergmann, Judith Allen Brough, & David Shepard

Write With Me:
Partnering With Parents in Writing Instruction
Lynda Wade Sentz

Family Math Night:
Math Standards in Action
Jennifer Taylor-Cox

Family Math Night:
Middle School Math Standard in Action
Jennifer Taylor-Cox & Christine Oberdorf

Activities, Games, and Assessment Strategies
for the Foreign Language Classroom
Amy Buttner

100 Games and Activities
for the Introductory Foreign Language Classroom
Thierry Boucquey

What Great Teachers Do *Differently*:
17 Things That Matter Most
(2nd Edition)
Todd Whitaker

Classroom Motivation for A to Z:
How to Engage Your Students in Learning
Barbara R. Blackburn

Dealing With *Difficult* Parents:
And With Parents In Difficult Situations
Todd Whitaker & Douglas J. Fiore

Supplemental Downloads

Many of the tools discussed and displayed in this book are also available on the Routledge website as Adobe Acrobat files. Permission has been granted to purchasers of this book to download these tools and print them.

You can access these downloads by visiting www.routledge.com/9781596672109 and click on the Free Downloads tab.

Index of Free Downloads

About the Authors

Darcy J. Hutchins, Ph.D. in education policy studies from the University of Maryland-College Park, is Senior Program Facilitator with the National Network of Partnership Schools (NNPS) at Johns Hopkins University. She provides professional development that enables district, state, and organization leaders and school teams to establish and maintain comprehensive partnership programs to increase student success. She is co-author of *Family Reading Night* (Hutchins, et al., Eye On Education, 2008) and *School, Family, and Community Partnerships: Your Handbook for Action, Third Edition* (Epstein, et al., Corwin Press, 2009). She is also lead editor of annual books of *Promising Partnership Practices* published by NNPS. She is co-author of a chapter on family involvement in the middle grades, published by the Association for Middle Level Education (2012).

Marsha D. Greenfeld is Senior Program Facilitator with the National Network of Partnership Schools (NNPS) at Johns Hopkins University. She provides professional development to help leaders in districts, states, and organizations and school teams implement and sustain goal-linked programs of family and community involvement. She is co-author of *Family Reading Night* (Hutchins, et al., Eye On Education, 2008) and *School, Family, and Community Partnerships: Your Handbook for Action, Third Edition* (Epstein, et al., Corwin Press, 2009). She also is a co-editor of annual books of *Promising Partnership Practices*, published by NNPS. Previously, Ms. Greenfeld was a teacher and district-level facilitator for partnerships in the Baltimore City School System, worked with the Office of Federal Grants Programs in Washington D.C. Public Schools, and was a partnership coordinator with Communities in Schools.

Joyce L. Epstein, Ph.D. in sociology from Johns Hopkins University, is Director of the Center on School, Family, and Community Partnerships, Principal Research Scientist, and Research Professor of Sociology at Johns Hopkins University. In 1995, she established the National Network of Partnership Schools (NNPS) to help school, district, and state leaders develop research-based programs of family and community involvement. Dr. Epstein has over one hundred publications on the nature and effects of family and community involvement. These include *School, Family, and Community Partnerships: Your Handbook for Action, Third Edition* (Epstein, et al., Corwin Press, 2009), and a textbook for college courses for future teachers and administrators, *School, Family, and Community Partnerships: Preparing Educators and Improving Schools, Second Edition* (Westview, 2011). She was named a Fellow of the American Educational Research Association (AERA) in 2009 and received the 2009 Elizabeth Cohen Award from AERA's Sociology of Education Special Interest Group.

Mavis G. Sanders, Ph.D. in education from Stanford University, is Professor of Education at the University of Maryland-Baltimore County and Senior Advisor to NNPS at Johns Hopkins University. She is the author of many publications on how schools and districts develop their partnership programs and effects of partnerships on African-American adolescents' school success. Her most recent book, *Principals Matter: A Guide to School, Family, and Community Partnerships* (with Steven Sheldon, Corwin Press, 2009) focuses on principals' leadership for developing effective partnership programs. She is co-author of *School, Family, and Community Partnerships: Your Handbook for Action, Third Edition* (Epstein, et al., Corwin Press, 2009). Other books include *Building School-Community Partnerships: Collaboration for Student Success*, (Corwin Press, 2005), and *Schooling Students Placed at Risk* (LEA, 2000). A new article, "Achieving scale at the district level: A longitudinal multiple case study of a partnership reform," will appear in *Educational Administration Quarterly* (in press).

Claudia L. Galindo, Ph.D. in education policy and comparative international education from Penn State University, is Assistant Professor of Language, Literacy, and Culture at the University of Maryland-Baltimore County. She is a specialist in research on issues of educational inequality, minority students' educational experiences, and Hispanic students and families and has authored many papers on these topics. Dr. Galindo is co-author (with Epstein and Sheldon) on an article, "Levels of leadership: Effects of district and school leaders on the quality of school programs of family and community involvement," (2011) in *Education Administration Quarterly*. She is co-author of "Examining the effects of school and home connections on children's kindergarten cognitive growth," to appear in *Early Childhood Research Quarterly*. She served as a section editor and author on family and community involvement for the *Encyclopedia of Diversity in Education* (edited by James Banks) to be published in 2012.

Preface

Fact: All parents influence their children's lives and learning in many ways.

Challenge: Not all parents are sure about how to help their children succeed in school at each grade level.

Fact: Teachers know that family and community involvement is important for students' success.

Challenge: Not all teachers are prepared to engage all parents and community partners in ways that support student learning and development.

Fact: Just about all schools today serve diverse populations of students and their families.

Challenge: Not all schools have effective programs and practices to communicate and collaborate with parents of diverse educational, economic, racial, ethnic, linguistic, and cultural backgrounds.

Fact: Scores of research studies confirm that when their parents are involved in their education, children from culturally diverse and economically stressed families are more likely to succeed in school.

Challenge: It is not always clear how to apply research results in practice.

What do these facts and challenges mean for improving school, family, and community partnerships? This information is discussed in many books, but actions are needed to solve these challenges.

In order for all parents to remain positive influences in their children's education at every grade level, all schools must develop and maintain effective, equitable, and goal-linked programs of family and community involvement. This can be a difficult task—but we have found that educators, parents, and other partners in hundreds of schools in the National Network of Partnership Schools (NNPS) at Johns Hopkins University (2011) are eager and able to work together on productive partnerships.

This book takes a step-by-step approach to enable every elementary and middle school to increase the involvement of all parents—including immigrant and refugee parents—in their children's education at school and at home. The summary of research in Chapter 1, discussion of logistics in Chapter 2, and activities in Chapters 3 to 11 guide educators and parents to create a multicultural school that welcomes all families, respects their differences, and honors their common goals for student success.

The book also addresses a critical goal for student learning. In this world with its global economy, it is important for students to be internationally aware and educationally competitive with students from other countries. Students' knowledge about and interest in other nations and other cultures should be developed in the elementary grades and extended and strengthened as students progress through school. We believe that an interconnected world begins with a well-connected school, where teachers, parents, administrators, community partners, and students work together, appreciate each other, and strive for student success. If schools organize effective partnership programs with activities such as those presented in this book, students will increase their understanding and appreciation of different countries, rich cultures, exciting talents, and extensive resources that surround them in their schools, neighborhoods, and communities.

By taking action on this agenda—in YOUR school—more families will be engaged, more teachers will know and respect their students' families, and more students will be ready for the world.

Acknowledgments

The authors thank the schools whose creative activities to involve all families are featured in this book: El Rancho Elementary School, Chino Valley, CA; Highwood Hills Elementary School, St. Paul, MN; Isaac Stevens Middle School, Pasco, WA; L'Etoile du Nord French Immersion School, Saint Paul, MN; Patterson High School, Baltimore, MD; Ranch View Elementary School, Naperville, IL; Roger Wolcott Early Childhood Center, Windsor, CT; Ruth Livingston Elementary School, Pasco, WA; and Saeger Middle School, St. Charles, MO.

In various chapters we also cited wonderful activities conducted in other schools: Grove Elementary School, Wisconsin Rapids, WI; Highlands Elementary School, Naperville, IL; McLoughlin Middle School, Pasco, WA; and Meadow Glens Elementary School, Naperville, IL.

The featured activities in this book are just a few of the hundreds of excellent activities submitted by school and district members of the National Network of Partnership Schools at Johns Hopkins University. Their inspiring efforts—including many to engage diverse families and increase multicultural awareness—are published in annual books of *Promising Partnership Practices* (go to www.partnershipschools.org and click on the section Success Stories).

We thank four reviewers who provided thoughtful suggestions on an earlier version of this manuscript. They helped us improve all of the chapters. Many thanks, too, to Lorraine M. Landon for the Spanish translations in this book. Finally, we gratefully acknowledge a grant from MetLife Foundation to the Center on School, Family, and Community Partnerships at Johns Hopkins University, which supported our work on this book.

Darcy J. Hutchins
Marsha D. Greenfeld
Joyce L. Epstein
Johns Hopkins University
Center on School, Family, and Community Partnerships

Mavis G. Sanders
University of Maryland-Baltimore County
Department of Education

Claudia L. Galindo
University of Maryland-Baltimore County
Department of Language, Literacy, and Culture

Table of Contents

PART ONE

Introduction

Chapter 1: The Imperative: Schools Must Involve All Families

◆ Review a summary of decades of research on the nature and effects of involving immigrant families in their children's education.

◆ Learn about "the cultural iceberg" and "funds of knowledge" to understand all families' strengths.

◆ See recommendations to address the urgent agenda for school-based partnership programs that engage all families.

Chapter 2: The Logistics: How to Increase the Involvement of Multicultural Families in YOUR School

◆ Explore essentials for organizing activities for family nights, workshops, and curriculum connections to increase the involvement of families with diverse backgrounds at school and at home.

◆ Learn to form a planning committee, solve challenges that limit parents' participation, and engage families in ways that create a welcoming school climate and increase student success.

CHAPTER 1
The Imperative: Schools Must Involve All Families

Schools are multiplexes—multifaceted and complex places. Schools today serve students of many races, ethnicities, languages, cultures, religions, economic conditions, geographies, and other diversities. Students in U.S. schools are White, African American, Hispanic, Asian, Pacific Islander, Native American, and of other and mixed backgrounds.[1] They live in urban, suburban, and rural communities in families with more or less formal education and in varied socioeconomic situations. Students live with one or two parents, grandparents, foster parents, guardians, same sex parents, and other caregivers.[2] They include English Language Learners, gifted learners, and children with other learning differences and special needs.

Students and their families bring multiple and complex characteristics—across and within cultures—to every school every day. Their diversities hold many opportunities for enriching student learning and development. In this book, we present ideas to help schools recognize these resources and develop and implement practical activities that will increase the involvement of parents with different racial, ethnic, linguistic, and cultural backgrounds to create a welcoming school community and more successful students.[3]

Multicultural Schools

Diversity in U.S. schools increases by the day. Presently, more than 40 percent of all public school students are from diverse cultures—double the percentage in the 1980s. More than 20 percent are Hispanic students. The U.S. census predicts that by 2023, more than 50 percent of all public school students will be of Hispanic origin. This already is true in California and several other western states, making the so-called minority group a majority group in the public schools (CBS, 2011; National Center for Education Statistics, 2009).

There are significant variations in these numbers across states and cities. In Saint Paul Public Schools (2010) in Minnesota, for example, about 40 percent of students speak a primary home language other than English, with a large percentage of Hmong families. In Maryland, families come from more than 180 countries and speak more than 100 home languages (Han, 2010). In New York City, more than 60 percent of the district's one million public school students are immigrants or children of immigrants (Advocates for Children of New York, 2009), and about 15 percent of these students are classified as English Language Learners (Zehr, 2009).

This trend will continue. Large numbers of immigrant and refugee families will continue to come from Southeast and East Asia, South and Central America, Africa, the Caribbean, the Pacific Islands, and Europe to join the diverse population of students in the public schools (Fortuny, Hernandez, & Chaudry, 2010). The changing demographics in America's public schools and pressures to prepare students for participation in a global economy require educators to work with all families in new ways that guide and support all students to achieve their full potential at every grade level (Asia Society, 2010; Moll & Ruiz, 2002).

Federal education policies, including Title I, support this new direction by requiring educators to involve all families in ways that support student achievement and school success and by communicating in languages that parents understand. The policies reflect research conducted for several decades that shows that educators in preschools, elementary, middle, and high schools can and should take responsibility for organizing strong programs and practices to involve families in productive ways. Most states, districts, and schools set the same goals in their policies, recommendations, and mission statements. These policies that call for organized, goal-linked partnership programs must be implemented, not just recorded (Allen, 2007).

Challenges and Opportunities

Families that immigrate to the United States are diverse. Some are well educated and highly skilled, and, on average, their children achieve at high levels in schools in all parts of the country. Other students of new-immigrant families live in poor urban and rural communities. On average, these students attend under-resourced schools, experience high stress, have low achievement test scores, and are less likely to graduate from high school or attend and complete college (Suárez-Orozco, Rhodes, & Milburn, 2009). Students' low achievement is a real challenge that schools must address, but the same students and their families also bring a wealth of knowledge, talent, and other (sometimes hidden) resources to their schools and communities. Further, research suggests that the persistent achievement gaps between groups of students would close quicker if educators, parents, and community members worked better together to support students' attitudes about school and learning (Sheldon, 2009).

Educators have three choices. They can ignore diversity, complain about diversity, or recognize and use the richness in family cultures and backgrounds to increase student success in school. This book will help educators make the right choice.

What the Research Says

Students and Families Are Diverse Within and Across Groups

For more than thirty years, studies have reported that, on average, students from poor immigrant families tend to lag behind other students in reading, writing, math, science, and other school subjects. As important, researchers also consistently report that there is more diversity in achievement *within* groups than *between* groups. That is, some Latino students do better than others, and the same is true for students in all racial, ethnic, geographic, and socioeconomic groups (Reardon & Galindo, 2009; Suárez-Orozco & Suárez-Orozco, 2001). No group has a monopoly on high or low test scores or success in school. The variations are due to many preimmigration factors, including family income and education levels (Arzubiaga, Nogueron, & Sullivan, 2009).

Individual beliefs and behaviors also vary within groups. In fact, there is no monolithic Latino, African American, Asian, or European culture and no one way to characterize an entire group of students or families. Stereotypes are hard to eliminate, but educators must reject labels that define groups as if all members were the same. Within any racial or ethnic group, students and families differ in their skills, beliefs, values, goals, talents, needs, and resources (Adelman & Taylor, 2011; Delgado-Gaitan & Trueba, 1991).

Despite the diversity of characteristics within and across groups, there also are some important commonalities. Countless studies confirm that immigrant parents come to the United States with hopes and dreams for their children's education. Just about all families love their children, value education, and want their children to succeed in school and in life (Chavez, 2007; Delgado-Gaitan, 2004; Delpit, 1995; Etzioni, 2003). No family sends a child to school to fail.

Still, parents vary in their readiness for involvement in education. Many immigrant families are unfamiliar with U.S. schools and unsure of their roles in their children's education at different grade levels (Northeast and Islands Regional Educational Laboratory, 2002). Many parents speak and read the language of their home country, even as they and their children learn English to assimilate in a new land. Some come to the United States with the belief that it is disrespectful for parents to question—or even converse with—educators. Although they may not be ready to take leadership roles with educators, most parents are eager and able to support their children as students in U.S. schools (Advocates for Children of New York, 2009; Dauber & Epstein, 1993; Delgado-Gaitan, 2004).

The research results seem contradictory and raise critical questions. Do immigrant students and families have special needs or are they similar to other families? Although individuals differ within groups, do families from the same country or region bring with them customs, beliefs, languages, and histories that they want to preserve and share? Why is it important for educators to learn about and celebrate the richness of each culture of the students and families in a school?

Schools Vary in the Quality of Their Partnership Programs
Studies conducted over the past two decades found that many schools are not prepared to work collaboratively with diverse families (Chavkin, 1993; Chavkin & Gonzalez, 1995; Epstein & Dauber, 1991; Waterman & Harry, 2008). Surveys and interviews show that some teachers and administrators believe that "those parents" do not care about education. Despite data to the contrary from parents, some educators ignore, exclude, or blame parents who are "hard to reach" and who are not present at school activities and events.

Historically, parental involvement has been left up to the parents, unplanned, and not formally evaluated. New research shows that programs of school, family, and community partnerships are up to the schools—an official part of district, school, and classroom organization (Adelman & Taylor, 2011; Chrispeels & Rivero, 2001; Epstein, 2011; Epstein, Galindo, & Sheldon, 2011; Epstein & Sheldon, 2006; Henderson, Mapp, Johnson, & Davies, 2007; Marsh & Turner-Vorbeck, 2009; Rodriguez-Brown, 2009; Weiss, Lopez, & Rosenberg, 2010). Indeed, most educators say that they want to involve diverse parents—indeed, all parents—but do not know how to do so (Epstein, 2011; MetLife, 2010). It is time to move on from these old stories and take new directions to develop and sustain equitable and effective programs of family and community involvement.

The good news is that researchers and educators have been working together to learn *how* to organize partnership programs in highly diverse communities (Kugler, 2012). Structures and processes have been developed and tested with thousands of educators across the country in schools that serve highly diverse families (Epstein et al., 2009). By using research-based approaches, districts and schools are improving the organization and progress of their programs of family and community involvement.

Educators must *know their students' families.* They may use background data collected by the school, as well as information that students and parents provide in surveys, interviews, and formal or informal meetings. In each school, a team of educators, parents of all backgrounds, and community partners must work together to select and implement practices of family and community involvement that match parents' backgrounds, interests, and abilities and that contribute to goals for school improvement and student success (Allen, 2007; Boethel, 2003; Epstein et al., 2009; Galindo, in press; Jordan, 2002; Stepanek & Raphael, 2010).

Summary of Research

The results of decades of studies on immigrant families and on schools' partnership programs confirm important facts.

What does research say about the involvement of immigrant families in children's education?

◆ Immigrant parents, like all parents, love their children and care about their education.

◆ There are important differences within groups that prohibit educators from stereotyping any cultural group of students or families.

◆ Immigrant families bring important knowledge, talents, and other resources from their home countries that can enrich the school curriculum, increase students' self-confidence, and help educators and parents understand each other and their roles in children's education.

◆ New immigrant and refugee parents may be wary of the school and unfamiliar with the policies and expectations of schools in the United States. They may benefit from connections with parents who speak their home language to become more confident participants in their children's education.

What does research say about school programs to involve immigrant (and all) families in their children's education?

◆ All schools serve students and families with diverse backgrounds and characteristics.

◆ Teachers, principals, counselors, and other educators know that good teaching is not enough to ensure student learning and development. They know that they must involve all families in their children's education, but many are not sure how to do so.

◆ Educators and researchers have designed and tested structures and processes that enable schools at all levels to engage all families in feasible ways that benefit students.

Recommendations: Across many studies of diverse populations, researchers list the same five major recommendations to increase the involvement of immigrant and refugee families in their children's education at school and at home:

◆ **Welcome all families.** Parents need to know that educators understand, value, and respect the work they do to care for their children and their efforts to guide them to succeed in school.

◆ **Communicate in languages that parents understand.** Schools must demonstrate that they are ready and able to communicate with all families. This starts with clear English language in memos, notices, computerized phone messages, report cards, and in meetings with parents. This also may require translators and interpreters to connect with parents with different primary home languages.

Translation services may be provided by the district office, parent volunteers, high school students in service learning programs, or community organizations and citizen volunteers. Every year, more immigrant parents become bilingual in their home language and English (Mancilla-Martinez & Kieffer, 2010). This creates a stream of potential translators and interpreters who may help other parents feel welcome at meetings and events and part of the school community.

◆ **Provide parents with clear, useful, and timely information about the school and school system.** All parents—and, especially, parents who did not attend U.S. schools—need information on school policies, parents' rights to specific information, school and community programs open to their children, expectations for parental involvement, contact persons to answer questions about the school, and guidance from grade-level and classroom teachers on how to help their children each year.

◆ **Organize a planned program of activities that enables all parents to be productively involved in their children's education at school and/or at home.** Educators at the district and school levels must be intentional and purposeful about ensuring equity in opportunities for family involvement. They must understand that it is their professional responsibility to organize, implement, evaluate, and continually improve school-based programs of family and community involvement. Only in this way will it be possible to involve all families—including immigrant and refugee families—so that all students are supported by home, school, and community to do their best in school.

◆ **Incorporate students' backgrounds and family cultures into the classroom curricula and in the school's program of family and community involvement.** Teachers may use family and community knowledge and resources to enrich the curriculum and instruction to boost students' learning. Educators and parents must work together to incorporate the richness of diverse cultures in family and community involvement activities to increase the participation of many families who were not previously involved at school or at home in their children's education.

By enacting these recommendations, any school can attain the competing goals of developing a unified school community and meeting the specific needs and concerns of families with diverse economic, racial, ethnic, and linguistic backgrounds (Nieto & Bode, 2011). As school-based partnership programs improve, all families— including racially and culturally diverse families—will become more engaged in their children's education at school and at home.

Understanding Family Cultures

To understand students' families and cultural backgrounds, educators must meet and talk with parents, students, and others in the community and study their countries of origin. Personal connections and some reading will help educators understand the history and culture of each group in the school (Banks & Banks, 2004; Gay, 2000).

Cultural Iceberg

A diagram of an iceberg often is used to display the complex structure of culture (derived from Hall, 1976; http://www.culturaliceberg.com). It is said that, like an iceberg, about 10 percent of the customs, values, and beliefs of any culture is *visible* and *public* and about 90 percent is *hidden* or *covert* and requires intensive study, as shown in the following figure.

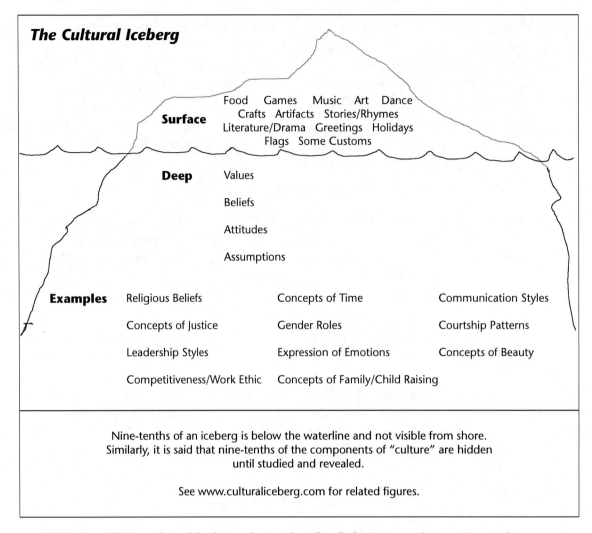

The Cultural Iceberg

Surface
Food   Games   Music   Art   Dance
Crafts   Artifacts   Stories/Rhymes
Literature/Drama   Greetings   Holidays
Flags   Some Customs

Deep
Values

Beliefs

Attitudes

Assumptions

Examples

Religious Beliefs	Concepts of Time	Communication Styles
Concepts of Justice	Gender Roles	Courtship Patterns
Leadership Styles	Expression of Emotions	Concepts of Beauty
Competitiveness/Work Ethic	Concepts of Family/Child Raising	

Nine-tenths of an iceberg is below the waterline and not visible from shore.
Similarly, it is said that nine-tenths of the components of "culture" are hidden
until studied and revealed.

See www.culturaliceberg.com for related figures.

The top of the cultural iceberg shows that food, dress, greetings, art, music, games, literature, holidays, rituals, manners, and other features are overt or visible features of a culture. Below the surface are values, beliefs, attitudes, and assumptions including religious beliefs, ideas about beauty and modesty, concepts of justice, attitudes about time, nonverbal communications such as patterns of smiling and eye contact, and other covert or private features of a culture. Knowledge and understanding of hidden cultural qualities develop over time through study, frequent communications, shared activities, and friendships that permit discussions of deep and often emotional issues.

What is "authentic" about culture? To involve more and diverse families, educators often start by featuring the visible and public components of culture to help all students and families feel welcome at school (e.g., welcome signs in all languages of the school's families; multicultural fairs that feature families' countries of origin). Well-planned activities enable parents and students to share family stories, nursery rhymes, songs, dances, crafts, skits, food, holiday traditions, costumes, flags, photographs, and artifacts. First steps of welcome, celebration, and relationship-building increase the involvement of families who may have, initially, felt excluded from the school (Allen, 2007; Hutchins et al., 2011).

Some have criticized these activities as lacking authenticity, but all aspects of a culture—visible and invisible, overt and covert—may be authentic and important, depending on the stated goals for an activity. Indeed, even as they work to become part of their adopted country, families strive to maintain and share things they love about their culture—food, language, and other memories of home (Gong, 2008; Wilkerson, 2010).

Every student's family culture is rooted in languages, idioms, geography, stories, music, and other social and historic factors. By sharing and celebrating these and other customs, teachers and students learn about the diverse cultures in the school. Parents meet teachers and learn more about their children's schools. After focusing on the visible aspects of cultures, educators are more likely to advance to more challenging activities that integrate cultural components in the curriculum to advance students' learning (Galindo, in press; Richardson, 2011).

First steps in partnership program development build a base of good connections, clear communications, and positive attitudes—all needed to establish mutual respect and trust among educators and families with diverse backgrounds. First steps must be followed by many next steps to help educators, parents, students, and community partners build a caring school community that supports all students' success in school (Sleeter & Grant, 2003).

Funds of Knowledge

Many researchers have urged educators to incorporate students' backgrounds and family resources into the curriculum to increase student learning (Banks & Banks, 2004; Northeast and Islands Regional Educational Laboratory, 2002). Teachers are advised to use *culturally responsive, culturally relevant*, and *culturally sensitive* approaches in their classrooms (Delgado-Gaitan, 2006; Gay, 2002; Ladson-Billings, 1995, 2004). These usually entail:

◆ Learning about and referring to students' home cultures so that students see some clear connections between school skills and their family life.

◆ Tapping the skills and resources of parents' and community members from different racial, ethnic, linguistic, and cultural groups to enrich the curriculum, expand students' experiences, and enhance student learning.

◆ Connecting families from diverse cultures with other parents who speak the same language so that immigrant parents feel welcome at school, expand their social networks, participate in family involvement activities and events, and become more involved in their children's education.

In visits and discussions with students' parents, teachers learn about parents' skills and talents or *funds of knowledge* (Gonzalez, Moll, & Amanti, 2005; Moll, Amanti, Neff, & Gonzalez, 1992; Valdes, 1996) in art, music, storytelling, farming, carpentry, medicine, shopkeeping, cooking, sports, gardening, and countless other areas. Teachers may use this information to spark conversations with students so that school skills relate to family backgrounds, invite parents into the classroom to discuss or demonstrate skills that enrich specific units of work or projects, and design homework that guides students to talk with or interview parents about their homelands and experiences.

Families' funds of knowledge also may help educators strengthen their programs of family and community involvement (Allen, 2007; Galindo, in press; Stepanek & Raphael, 2010). Teachers may call upon parents to conduct workshops for other parents, participate in forums to discuss ideas for school improvement, and connect with other parents to support partnership activities.

Parents also have funds of knowledge about their own child's talents, strengths, and needs. Through phone calls, notes, e-mail, and parent-teacher conferences conducted in any language, parents may provide information about their children that teachers can use to motivate students' learning and development.

Communities have funds of knowledge that teachers and families can tap. Indeed, a good partnership program connects school and home with businesses, social service agencies, faith-based organizations, and other community groups and citizens. Multicultural, ethnic, and multilingual groceries, eateries, media (newspapers, radio, TV, cable), and other community-based organizations (CBOs) all have resources that may increase the involvement of diverse families in their children's education (Sanders, 2006). Community resources strengthen school programs; assist students with tutors, mentors, internships, and other learning opportunities; and offer services that improve the quality of family life.

In sum, educators may incorporate diverse cultures into the curriculum and school life in many ways, from simple, visible activities (e.g., posting welcome signs in the school lobby in all families' languages; creating family photo walls or displays of art from many nations) to complex activities (e.g., having students interview family and community members about their memories of their home countries and the experience of immigration; inviting family and community members as speakers in class).

Two-Way Cultural Exchanges

In successful programs of family and community involvement, information flows in two directions.

◆ Educators learn more about students' families and communities, find ways to communicate in languages parents understand, and communicate useful and timely information about the school and their child's educational program.

◆ Parents learn more about the school, teachers' expectations for their children, the school's program of family and community involvement, and the roles parents play in helping their children do their very best in school.

This two-way exchange applies to all teachers and all parents, but special attention is needed to engage new immigrant and refugee parents who may have been excluded in the past and who are unfamiliar with the organization of their children's schools. When two-way connections are made, more and different parents—indeed, all parents—may become involved in positive ways.

Conclusion: An Urgent Agenda

Despite strong agreement about the importance of family involvement and the need to reach out to immigrant and refugee parents, too many districts and schools have lagged in developing effective partnership programs. Parents have been left on their own to figure out how to become involved with their children at each grade level. This kind of benign neglect does not meet the needs of students, families, or schools.

An urgent agenda has been set for students and for educators in districts and schools across the country in order to close achievement gaps between groups of students and enable all students to complete high school, prepare for college or work, and meet their full potential. To reach these goals for student learning, all available resources are needed—good teachers, engaged families, and committed communities. Schools must sort through the multiple complexities discussed above and take action to develop inclusive programs that engage all families and the community in ways that support student success in school. When students see that their teachers and parents communicate and work together, more students—including those in immigrant families—will take their schoolwork seriously. More will know that their schoolwork is valued at home and their family culture is valued at school.

About This Book

This book aims to help educators in elementary and middle schools engage immigrant and culturally diverse families—indeed, all families—in their children's education. In so doing, educators will learn more about students' families, families will learn more about the schools, and, thanks to these connections, youngsters will feel more comfortable and confident in the role of student.

We selected three strategies—Multicultural Family Nights, Workshops for Parents, and Curriculum Connections—that enable educators and parents to work together in different ways to improve the school climate, strengthen families' connections to the school, and increase student success. For each strategy, basic and advanced activities are outlined with simple directions and creative variations. The featured activities, developed for elementary and middle schools, may be replicated or adapted for other school levels and for local populations.[4]

Chapter 2 offers useful suggestions for organizing activities to increase the involvement of families with diverse backgrounds at school and at home. This process starts by creating a planning committee or team of teachers, parents, administrators, and community partners to write good plans to engage all families, organize meetings, schedule activities, and evaluate their efforts.[5]

Chapter 2 provides ideas to solve common challenges in reaching out to multicultural families and successfully implementing involvement activities. For example, school leaders or planning committees may first survey parents to determine their interests, preferences, and students' needs. Parents may recommend that the school conduct a family night or workshop on how to help their children at home in a particular subject, or other involvement activities.[6] The parents also may indicate whether they would, in fact, participate in or lead the activities they have suggested. Ideas from diverse parents should help any school develop equitable and inclusive partnerships that focus on student success in school.

Family Nights

Family Nights are intergenerational programs that bring teachers, parents, students, grandparents, and other community members together for important and enjoyable learning activities. Some family nights are designed to feature multicultural customs, food, song, dance, and other contributions of different cultures to increase the participation of immigrant and refugee parents—along with all families at the school.

Here, we introduce three ways to organize Multicultural Family Nights—focused on art (Chapter 3), games (Chapter 4), and cultures-by-country (Chapter 5) to attract large numbers of students, family members, and teachers and to show that the school values and celebrates the diverse cultures of its students.

Family nights may be held at the school building or in the community. Although often conducted in the early evening with dinner for the participants, family events also may be conducted during the day before school, after school, or during lunch. Whenever they are scheduled, translators and interpreters may be needed to ensure that all families can participate and enjoy the activities.

Family nights, designed to welcome students and parents to the school, may spotlight important topics that students are studying in class, demonstrate ways for students and parents to work together at the event and at home, or feature topics of interest or importance for everyone (e.g., Cinco de Mayo or Hmong New Year; health and exercise; summer programs; the love of reading). Multicultural Family Nights may be organized by parents to feature their own family cultures or developed by students and teachers to present information and activities on a country studied in class.

In all of these ways, students learn that their teachers recognize their families' cultures and that their families support student success in school. Family nights that feature the visible, comfortable components of diverse cultures may help a school start to develop its partnership program.

Workshops for Parents

Workshops for parents are well-planned meetings where parents and other caregivers can gain information and skills, ask questions, offer opinions to educators, and share knowledge with other parents and with educators. There are many designs for workshops, which must be on topics of interest to parents and of importance for school programs and student success.

Here, we introduce three ways to organize workshops: as a *forum* where parents can contribute ideas for school improvement (Chapter 6); as a *series* to build parents' knowledge and confidence about guiding their children through school and participating in school improvement (Chapter 7); and as a *redefined workshop* that guides parents in helping their children at home without requiring the parents to come to the school building (Chapter 8).

Schools use tear-offs, surveys, e-mails, focus groups, and informal conversations to solicit ideas from parents on workshop topics of interest. Workshop planners also need to know when parents can attend workshops—before school starts, morning, noon, afternoon, evening, or weekend hours. New technologies may permit parents to attend from a distance in web conferences or go-to meetings.

Some workshops for parents are organized as one-time meetings lasting from one hour to one full day, whereas others are scheduled as a series of two or more sessions. A full "course" at a "parent university" or "academy" may culminate with a closing or graduation ceremony. Workshops may be presented by school or district staff, parent leaders, community members, or outside experts. They may be conducted at a school or in the community.

Common topics are aspects of child and adolescent development (e.g., peer pressure; preventing bullying, drug abuse, or gang behavior); key transition points and parenting challenges (e.g., transitioning from elementary to middle school); school policies and programs (e.g., understanding the report card, helping a child with homework); and community resources (e.g., part-time jobs for teens, summer learning opportunities, ESL classes for parents).

Workshops must be conducted in languages that parents understand, with translators and interpreters, as needed, so that all parents who are interested may participate. There are variations on this theme. For example, one school elected to conduct a workshop for parents in Spanish, requiring the English speakers to use headphones for instant translations that night (see Chapter 6).

Some workshops and forums are designed for all families, whereas others are targeted for specific racial or ethnic groups to discuss particular topics or concerns (e.g., African American Parents Group, Hispanic Parents Group Forum, Hmong Parents Night). These meetings encourage frank talks with educators, problem solving, and personalized attention that increases parents' comfort with the school. These experiences often encourage parents to participate in other involvement activities with all other parents at the school.

Curriculum Connections

Curriculum Connections extend teachers' lessons by engaging parents, other family members, and/or community partners with students in learning activities at school or at home. Connections with the curriculum enable parents to celebrate, reinforce, or shape what students are learning in specific subjects. Here, we describe family involvement with students in culminating activities at the end of major units of work in different subjects (Chapter 9), in helping students learn family history (Chapter 10), and in reading with students at home (Chapter 11).

Curriculum Connections take many forms. Some shine a spotlight on students' work, new skills, and end-of-unit projects. Others draw on parents' funds of knowledge in classroom presentations and demonstrations.

Still other connections with the curriculum focus on homework—a natural connector of school and home (Epstein & Van Voorhis, 2001). Teachers may design homework that guides parents in how to help students practice a skill, read for pleasure, or complete other assignments or projects. Or students may conduct interactions with a parent or other family or community member. Using any language spoken at home, students may share something interesting they are learning in class; conduct a conversation, interview, or oral history on an interesting topic; complete a special project; or lead other activities with a family partner. Teachers may ask students to explore family stories of their home country, describe a family ancestor, ask about a parent's school or work experience, use family photographs to spark students' reading and writing, design a family flag, map the geographic path of the family's immigration, or conduct other engaging activities. Curriculum Connections ensure that parents see examples of students' work and increase their understanding of what teachers teach and what students learn in school.

Each part of the book—Multicultural Family Nights, Workshops for Parents, and Curriculum Connections—contains three chapters. Each chapter presents the following.

◆ **Featured Activity.** This section features a promising practice that has been successfully implemented in a school to increase the involvement of diverse families and to improve the quality of the school's partnership program.

◆ **You Try It.** This section discusses logistics to consider prior to implementing the featured activity. The ideas should help planning committees conduct or adapt the featured activity in their own schools with diverse families.

◆ **A Different Design.** This section describes another way to address the same goal as the featured activity, with step-by-step directions to engage diverse families and the community in children's education. The discussion covers the purpose, materials, planning, and follow-up needed to implement the different design.

◆ **Reproducibles.** Each chapter and the Appendix include reproducible documents, planning guides, handouts, and/or evaluation forms to help readers plan and implement the suggested activities. Most reproducibles are provided in English and Spanish.

The authors designed this book to help readers take action to increase the involvement of immigrant and all families in their children's education. Educators, parents, and community partners will have more ideas to improve the involvement of their students' families. Readers are invited to communicate with the authors to describe how they use or adapt activities in this book to address this urgent agenda.[7]

Chapter Notes

1. The U.S. census identifies ethnicity (i.e., Hispanic, Latino, or Spanish origin or non-Hispanic) and race separately. Here, we use the common categories that schools use to describe their student populations (White, African American, Hispanic or Latino, Asian, Pacific Islander, American Indian, and more than one or mixed race or ethnicity). Students and families may self-identify by ethnicity, race, religion, and/or country of origin.

2. Throughout this book, the word *parent* refers to the person or persons who are raising a school-age child and have the most contact with the school about the child's education and development. School programs of family and community involvement reach out to inform and engage parents, stepparents, foster parents, guardians, grandparents, other family members, and community partners who support children's learning.

3. Students and families are diverse in many ways. In this book, we aim to help schools reach out to involve families of different racial, ethnic, linguistic, and cultural backgrounds at all socioeconomic levels. We are particularly interested in how schools increase the involvement of immigrant, refugee, and migrant families (Arzubiaga, Nogueron, & Sullivan, 2009), as well as other families who are not presently involved at school or in their children's education. Examples in each chapter may focus on one racial or ethnic group, but the suggestions show how to extend or adapt the activities to engage many different family groups.

4. More examples of school-tested activities that create a welcoming school climate for all families and improve student attendance, behavior, and achievement can be found in the annual books of *Promising Partnership Practices* (Hutchins et al., 2011) and at www.partnershipschools.org in the Success Stories section of the website.

5. The three strategies and activities featured in this book are part of a comprehensive partnership program. In a full program, a district-level leader for partnerships guides school-based Action Teams for Partnerships (ATPs) to write annual action plans for family and community involvement linked to each school's improvement goals. The ATP is guided by a framework of six types of involvement: Type 1–parenting, Type 2–communicating, Type 3–volunteering, Type 4–learning at home, Type 5–decision making, and Type 6–collaborating with the community (Epstein, 1995; Epstein et al., 2009). By activating this framework, an ATP ensures that the school creates a welcoming environment and that parents can be involved at school, at home, or in the community in ways that help students enhance their reading, math, science, or other skills; improve attendance and behavior; plan for postsecondary education and training; and achieve other school goals.

    When a comprehensive partnership program is in place, teachers are less likely to stereotype parents who cannot attend school meetings. They know that all parents can be involved in other, helpful ways at home and in the community. Not all parents want to be parent leaders on school committees, but if the school provides timely and clear information, all parents can guide their children's development across the grades.

The ATP schedules, implements, delegates, or accounts for the implementation of goal-linked involvement activities to improve student attitudes, behaviors, and learning. The ATP also evaluates the quality of outreach, responses of parents, and results for students, and aims to improve its plans and practices each year. For details on how to develop a full partnership program, see Epstein et al. (2009) and the National Network of Partnership Schools at Johns Hopkins University (2011) (www.partnershipschools.org). In this book, we recommend a *planning committee* that will design and implement activities to engage diverse families in their children's education at school and at home (see Chapter 2). When a school is ready to develop a comprehensive partnership program, the planning committee may be transformed into a full ATP that will take responsibility for the broad agenda of involving all parents in ways that create a welcoming school climate and contribute to the academic and behavioral goals for student success in the school improvement plan.

6. The three featured approaches—Family Nights, Workshops for Parents, and Curriculum Connections—are not the only ways to engage multicultural families in their children's education. Two other strategies are popular in schools across the country to engage families with diverse backgrounds.

Home visits. There are many ways to organize home visits for teachers to meet and talk with parents in their own homes or in their neighborhoods. Home visits can be helpful to parents who are hesitant or unable to come to the school building. This activity emphasizes Type 1 involvement (parenting), with discussions of family and school goals, parents' interests and talents, how parents can conduct preschool reading and math readiness activities before enrolling their child in school, how teachers and parents can work together to advance student learning at any grade level, community programs for parents (e.g., GED, ESL), and many other topics.

It should be noted, however, that home visits may be time-consuming for teachers, expensive for districts that have to pay for teachers' time, and awkward for some parents who are uncomfortable about having teachers in their homes. Some teachers modify the idea of home visits by meeting parents at the children's school bus stop in their neighborhoods prior to the start of the school year, or in other community locations. They do this to reduce the cost of individual home visits while retaining the benefits of personal outreach to meet and greet parents in their own locations.

Given adequate funds and time, home visits are a viable strategy for increasing the involvement of parents who might otherwise remain distant from the school. Home visits also set the stage for parents and teachers to feel comfortable about conducting follow-up communications by phone or e-mail, without parents having to come to the school building.

Decision making. Many schools are aware of the need to diversify the representation of parents on school committees, councils, ATPs, and PTA/PTO committees. Attention to the representation of parent leaders emphasizes Type 5 involvement (decision making). All major groups of families in a school should have a voice on major committees so that all parents have a contact person who is interested in their input to school plans, programs, and decisions that affect their children. See Chapters 6–8 for preliminary steps to identify parent leaders from diverse cultures for decision-making committees.

There are, in fact, hundreds of activities—basic and complex—to activate the six types of involvement in ways linked to specific academic and behavioral goals (Epstein et al., 2009; Hutchins et al., 2011; National Network of Partnership Schools, 2011).

7. Readers may share their uses and adaptations of activities in this book with the authors via e-mail at nnps@jhu.edu.

CHAPTER 2
The Logistics: How to Increase the Involvement of Multicultural Families in YOUR School

It is clear from countless studies and field experiences summarized in Chapter 1 that increasing the involvement of multicultural families is a good idea for increasing their children's success in school. Some difficult questions, however, remain:

◆ How can every school achieve the goal of more equitable, inclusive, and productive family involvement?

◆ How can every school ensure that involvement activities are well designed, have high participation, and yield positive results for students?

This chapter answers a number of common questions that educators and teams of teachers, parents, and administrators have asked about organizing activities to involve families with diverse cultural backgrounds.

How should multicultural partnership activities be designed?

Schools across the United States conduct multicultural partnership activities in many different ways. This book focuses on three strategies that will enrich a school's partnership program.

◆ Multicultural Family Nights

◆ Workshops for Parents

◆ Curriculum Connections

Multicultural Family Nights enable students and their families to learn about different cultures through historical representations and traditions such as song, dance, food, and holidays. Often, Multicultural Family Nights are organized with country-specific booths or stations that offer various experiences or activities. Students may receive a "passport" that they and their family members take to the "countries" they visit. When they conduct an activity in that country, the passport is stamped and may be entered in a lottery or drawing for a celebratory prize at the end of the evening.

Some schools ask parents, other family members, or community groups to prepare displays or activities about their home countries. Other schools ask students to feature a country they studied in class.

Before conducting a Multicultural Family Night, a planning committee should consider which cultures are represented in the school, what the educators want students to learn about one another's heritage, and whether to organize the event around the school's different cultures or the countries that students study in class. See Chapters 3, 4, and 5 for several ideas.

Workshops for Parents give parents opportunities to meet and share ideas with other parents, learn new information, and discuss important topics for their children's development and success in school. Workshops may explain school policies, state tests, child and adolescent development, and help parents focus on specific issues such as preventing bullying and helping with homework.

Before conducting Workshops for Parents, a planning committee should gather advice from parents on topics they are interested in to ensure high attendance. In schools serving families from many nations, it is imperative to have interpreters at workshops so that parents who do not speak English can participate, and to have materials or handouts translated into languages parents can understand. Some schools provide headsets for instant translations in the parents' languages. See Chapters 6, 7, and 8 for several ways to organize effective Workshops for Parents.

Curriculum Connections begin in the classroom and then reach out to engage families and the community in ways that enrich or extend students' learning. Some schools use a Family Night or Workshop to describe the curriculum to parents (e.g., reading, math, writing, science) and explain how to support students' work and learning in specific subjects at home. Other schools organize activities for students to bring home and conduct with a family partner. These activities do not require a parent to come to the school building. To increase the involvement of multicultural families, teachers may design creative homework activities or projects that require students to talk with a family member about their home country, their experiences when they were the students' age, and other topics to help students learn about their family's culture and heritage.

Before implementing Curriculum Connections, the planning committee should meet with individual teachers or grade-level teams of teachers to discuss strategies for students to talk and work with their parents or other family partners on homework in specific subjects. Parents want to know how to "help" their child at home, but not how to "teach" every school subject. They enjoy celebrating student learning in different subjects. See Chapters 9, 10, and 11 for ways that teachers may engage diverse parents and community partners with students on learning activities at school and at home.

What is a planning committee and who should be on it?
Planning multicultural partnership activities is a team effort. Teachers, parents, and community members should work together as a planning committee to ensure that the activities welcome all families, respect families' values and beliefs, and benefit students.

A planning committee is led by a chair or co-chairs who oversee the group's efforts to write plans, schedule events, implement activities, and evaluate the quality of the work done. The committee may include teachers from each grade level and parent representatives from all major racial, ethnic, and cultural groups at the school. If a school serves Latino and African American students, the planning committee should include Latino and African American educators, parents, and other partners who connect and communicate with all parents in the school. Community partners (e.g., college students, school alumni, business partners, local sports figures) also may be on the planning committee or engaged in particular events.

The planning committee for improving multicultural partnership activities may be a subgroup of an Action Team for Partnerships (ATP)—teachers, parents, administrators, and others who work together to plan, implement, evaluate, and continually improve goal-linked family and community involvement activities that contribute to student success in school (Epstein et al., 2009). Like an ATP, the planning committee will select, outline, and schedule activities that reach out to engage multicultural families, increase the multicultural awareness and appreciation of all members of the school community, and support school improvement goals for student learning.

It is important for a team of educators, parents, and community partners—not one individual—to create this agenda so that diverse perspectives are heard and creative ideas develop. When team members share responsibilities for conducting involvement activities, they broaden participation by diverse families and strengthen the likelihood that the school will sustain its partnership program.

Which elements contribute to successful multicultural partnerships?

Each school must know its students and families. Each school must set its own goals for student improvement and success. Each school's program of family and community involvement activities will be different from the next. Yet there are some universal elements that will help any school—every school—increase the involvement of all parents in their children's education. A planning committee should consider the following elements to engage multicultural families and others who have been excluded or uninvolved in the past. In addition, each chapter of this book contains more suggestions for conducting specific activities and for improving outreach, participation, and results of family and community involvement.

Dinner. In most successful programs, activities held in the evening include a light dinner for volunteers and participants. Other activities during the day may include light snacks. Business partners often are willing to donate dinners for well-planned, goal-oriented events. Multicultural family nights may highlight foods of different cultures contributed by families or by local ethnic restaurants. Potluck dinners actively involve many families. In all cases, the planning committee must ensure that there is enough food for all participants who register to attend. It also must try to accommodate food restrictions or allergies.

Student and Family Performances. When students perform a song, dance, dramatic reading or play, debate, or other production, parents are more likely to attend. Similarly, when parents are asked to present something about their home countries or cultures, they are more likely to attend the event. Often, they will bring other family members and neighbors. Over the course of one school year, the planning committee should feature students and families from different grade levels in various ways to increase multicultural awareness and to encourage more and different families to attend.

Active Engagement. Few people enjoy sitting on hard chairs listening to someone lecture for two hours, especially in the evening after a busy day. Multicultural partnership activities should actively involve all participants in completing activities, sharing cultural values, conducting discussions, and celebrating successes. More parents will attend events that are active, enjoyable, informative, and culturally sensitive.

Publicity. It is essential to inform families about upcoming events in welcoming words and in languages that can be easily understood. Many schools send flyers, emails, or web-based notices to parents and note important activities on daily announcements to increase excitement among students. The planning committee may identify particular groups of parents to call or contact individually, using translators and interpreters as needed. The local media, including foreign language radio stations, newspapers, and cable TV channels, may help publicize multicultural family nights in public service announcements. Key community groups (e.g., faith-based organizations, neighborhood stores) may help disseminate information to families in parents' home languages. When parents receive good information and reminders about an event, they are more likely to attend.

Incentives. Some schools include surprises or prizes to encourage parents and students to participate in partnership activities. These include raffles and door prizes for parents and "No Homework" passes for students who attend with their families. Offering incentives—especially items linked to families' ethnicities and to student learning—adds spirit and purpose to the evening and shows participants that their attendance is appreciated.

Child Care. If educators want parents to attend an event at school, it may be necessary to provide child care for very young children. Ideally, the planning committee should select qualified adults to watch and work with toddlers of parents who attend Multicultural Family Nights and Workshops for Parents. Or teachers may supervise volunteers or teens performing service-learning activities to assist with child care. The school may provide age-appropriate books, movies, toys, or games in a child care room for very young children.

Transportation. Private or public transportation to school meetings and events may be a big problem for some families, especially those who are economically stressed or who live in neighborhoods far from the school. Many immigrant parents, particularly mothers and grandmothers, do not have a driver's license or access to a car. Some planning committees for increasing family involvement organize carpools, provide bus passes, or partner with faith-based institutions or van companies that have insurance and can transport people safely. Alternatively, schools may hold some meetings in community centers or housing complexes where large numbers of families live.

How can the community contribute to multicultural partnership activities?

Community organizations can be valuable partners for involving multicultural families in their children's education. Here are a few suggestions:

◆ The planning committee can ask local businesses, including restaurants, to donate meals, beverages, paper products, and other items for a well-planned, goal-oriented Multicultural Family Night or Workshop for Parents.

◆ Planners can identify groups or businesses that will offer items for door prizes, supplies for booths or activities, educational materials for children to take home, and other products for successful events.

◆ Planners can ask key community members from various ethnic groups to serve as guest speakers, sharing their backgrounds and both surface characteristics—food, dance, clothing, games, music—and deeper characteristics—values, beliefs, histories, and attitudes—of their home countries' cultures.

◆ Planners can publicize special events in the public library, local grocery stores, restaurants, and other community buildings.

◆ Planners can nurture connections in the community. School leaders should acknowledge the school's business and community partners in the publicity for events and in school newsletter articles after the activities. Planners can send thank you notes, issue certificates of appreciation, and celebrate community partners as school volunteers.

In good partnerships, the school, families, students, and community all benefit.

How can a planning committee prevent obstacles in order to increase the involvement of multicultural families?

Many challenges arise when educators and parents work together for student success. When one difficulty is solved, another challenge will emerge. That is, simply, the nature of school improvement. Additional challenges may occur in efforts to engage multicultural families at school and in students' learning due to language differences, parents' educational experiences in their homelands, and other situations. The planning committee should be ready to prevent some common obstacles from occurring in the first place and ensure that planned activities run smoothly and all families feel welcome.

Attend to language differences. The planning committee and all educators at a school should make sure that families receive information about their children's education and school activities and events in a language they understand. This may be English or a native language. Some districts have translation services that assist schools with this challenge. Other schools hire translators or invite multilingual parents to volunteer for this task. Schools or districts with large populations of non-English-speaking parents may offer courses to parents who would like to learn English. Similarly, schools may offer classes in Spanish (or other dominant languages) to English-speaking parents and teachers to help all leaders become bilingual.

Learn about cultural differences. Public schools in the United States were designed, traditionally, to serve White, middle-class families (Nieto & Bode, 2011; Woyshner,

2009). Today, the families in many schools do not fit that description. As a result, many multicultural families do not feel welcome at the school. They tend to shy away from events at the school building. Educators have a responsibility to learn about the families of the students, understand their cultures, learn their goals for their children, and demonstrate that the school is, indeed, a friendly place for all in the community. This goal—for educators to learn more about families' backgrounds—is assisted when the planning committee includes members from diverse cultures and starts with activities that do, in fact, welcome all families in positive, respectful, and fun-filled ways. The following chapters offer numerous examples of how schools may reach this goal.

Find time to plan activities and evaluate progress. Finding time for any school committee to meet is a challenge for busy teachers, administrators, and parents. Nevertheless, the planning committee should schedule at least one hour each month to plan an upcoming multicultural activity and to assess the quality of activities conducted in the previous month. Additional planning time may be needed by subgroups of the planning committee or other partners (e.g., teachers) to prepare for particular activities and major events. A sample planning page is provided in the Appendix to help the planning committee organize its work.

Teachers may be most involved in Curriculum Connections that engage students and parents on topics studied in class, including improving homework assignments that guide students to talk with a family member about their home countries (see Chapters 9, 10, and 11). By contrast, Multicultural Family Nights and Workshops for Parents require a team effort. Leadership for these activities may be distributed so that small groups or subcommittees of teachers, parents, administrators, and others can meet together, develop plans, and see that the activities are well implemented.

At each activity, a sign-in page will record attendance and an exit evaluation will gather reactions from all attendees. At each monthly meeting, the members of the planning committee should examine the reactions of attendees and discuss their own views of the quality of teamwork, support, outreach, and results of the activity. A sample sign-in sheet, exit evaluation, and planning team evaluation form for each activity are in the Appendix.

The chair or co-chairs of the planning committee must keep everyone up to date on progress made, needed assistance, next steps, and next meetings. Summaries of planning committee meetings should be sent to members who were unable to attend.

Avoid scheduling conflicts. Schools and households are busy places. Often it is difficult to arrange times for families to be active participants in their children's education. The planning committee may consider varying the days and times of Multicultural Family Nights and Workshops for Parents—some in the day and some in the evening—so that different parents will be able to attend at least some of the activities. More will attend when they are alerted to the scheduled activities well in advance and reminded about the activity close to the scheduled time. Curriculum Connections are designed to involve parents with students at home, but may need to be scheduled on a weekend or over two or three days so that parents can find time to talk about their ideas, read books together, and interact on a homework assignment.

Meet budgetary limits. Funding is a common concern for schools across the country. As part of the planning process, the planning committee should estimate the costs of its planned activities and identify the sources of funding.

- ◆ In some schools, a percentage of Title I funds is set aside for parental involvement activities.

- ◆ In many schools, business partners, volunteers, and ethnic organizations will help fund well-planned activities to involve families in ways that increase student success, thereby compensating for schools' low budgets.

- ◆ The school's PTA (or PTO) may elect to co-sponsor and help conduct particular events and provide funds for food or supplies.

- ◆ Some schools ask participants to pay a dollar or other small sum per person for dinner.

- ◆ The proceeds from schools' bake sales, book fairs, and other fund-raisers that require parents' support could be used to support other activities to engage all families and students in productive ways.

- ◆ Schools may apply for grants from federal, state, and local funders for well-designed, goal-linked partnership activities.

- ◆ District leaders may list funding opportunities and business partners for schools to contact.

Identify volunteers for needed tasks. Many partnership activities, including those involving multicultural families, benefit from well-prepared volunteers. The planning committee may enlist others to help conduct Multicultural Family Nights, Workshops for Parents, and Curriculum Connections. In addition to translating materials and serving as interpreters, as noted above, volunteers may call parents to remind them about a scheduled event, greet parents, serve dinner, watch younger children, conduct workshop sessions, supervise game stations, clean up, or complete other tasks for specific activities. Often, teachers and staff volunteer to help with activities and tasks.

Some schools invite parents, community members, business partners, high school and college students, senior citizens, school alumni, and others to volunteer for specific involvement activities that are planned throughout the school year. These volunteers are particularly helpful in activities for multicultural families if they speak the same language, live in the same neighborhood, or hale from the same country of origin.

Before recruiting volunteers, the planning committee needs to be clear about the number of helpers needed for particular activities, the time involved, and the training necessary to ensure success. All volunteers should be recognized and thanked for their contributions.

Develop strategies to provide information to parents who could not attend school events. One common challenge that all schools encounter is that most parents cannot attend workshops at the school, nor can they attend every family night. Many parents are employed full or part-time during the school day. Others live at a distance, may not have available transportation, and may have other obligations on particular days or evenings when involvement activities are scheduled at the school. Many of these parents, however, want and need the information that was offered at the school event.

The planning committee must consider how to get information home from meetings and workshops to parents who could not attend. Some schools summarize an event in the school newsletter, make a video of the activity for the school website, or send summaries or the actual handouts home for parents who request them. They may ask volunteers to share information with groups of parents in their native language. It is important for the planning committee to consider common and creative ways to make sure that all parents have access to information shared at major involvement activities. See Chapter 8 for examples of activities that address this challenge.

The chapters that follow present ideas for increasing the involvement of multicultural and all families in Family Nights, Workshops for Parents, and Curriculum Connections for student learning. For other examples of how schools organize successful activities, see Hutchins (2011) and NNPS (www.partnershipschools.org).

PART TWO

Multicultural Family Nights

Multicultural Family Nights enable students and their families to learn about different cultures through song, dance, food, and other representations.

What people are saying:

This celebration provided the incentive for some families to enter the school for the first time. Not only did they come, but their participation in the evening was phenomenal. They helped their children dress in native attire, brought in artifacts from around the world, and shared them with other school and community members who attended. As they celebrated their identity, they taught others to appreciate the similarities and differences with their own heritage.

Pam Rodriguez, Action Team Co-Chair,
Saeger Middle School, St. Charles, Missouri

Chapter 3: Exploring the World Through the Arts

◆ *Arts Extravaganza* from Highwood Hills Elementary School in St. Paul, Minnesota, illustrates how one school celebrated its students' diversity.

◆ *Tiempos Felices: Arte, Danza, Música / Happy Times: Art, Dance, Music* is an alternate design that shows how a school can highlight one culture's various art forms in different areas of the school.

Chapter 4: Games People Play

◆ *Games from Around the World* from Ruth Livingston Elementary School in Pasco, Washington, demonstrates how one school hosted an evening of board games with an international twist for students and parents.

◆ *International Favorites: Games People Play* is an alternate design that illustrates how a school may organize a family night linked to the home countries of students' families during which family members teach their favorite childhood games to the students.

Chapter 5: A School of Many Nations

◆ *Celebration of Nations* from Saeger Middle School in St. Charles, Missouri, shows how one school brought together students, teachers, parents, and the community to celebrate the diverse backgrounds of Saeger's sixth, seventh, and eighth graders and their families.

◆ *Our Community's Place in the World* is an alternate design that explains how a school may explore diversity and cultural richness in the community.

CHAPTER 3
Exploring the World Through the Arts

Learning about other cultures opens a world of understanding to students, teachers, and families in a school. The visual and performing arts of all cultural groups not only are beautiful and entertaining, but also stimulate students' creativity, curiosity, imagination, and self-expression. Using the arts to spotlight a school's diverse cultures and talents is a way to motivate learning, develop students' talents, and build respect for others. The featured activity shows how one school used the arts to learn about the homelands of students' families.

Featured Activity Arts Extravaganza

Highwood Hills Elementary School in Saint Paul, Minnesota, serves diverse students with African American, Cambodian, Hmong, Japanese, Latino, Somali, and other heritages. Nearly two-thirds of the students in this school are English Language Learners (ELLs). To celebrate its diversity, the school created an *Arts Extravaganza Family Night* featuring fourth-, fifth-, and sixth-grade students and their families. This event showcased familial and cultural traditions, combining performances with hands-on interactions so that students could both observe and participate in many traditional activities.

A team of planners gathered ideas from teachers, students, parents, and others and called for volunteers to conduct activities, prepare materials, and assist in other ways. The school gym was set up with stations highlighting Hmong story cloths, Hmong New Year Balls, Japanese origami, Hispanic tissue flowers, piñatas, Guatemalan kites, and henna painting. There also were several ethnic food stations. A Cambodian musician—the father of one of the students—performed traditional music. The evening culminated with a participatory performance by a local African American storyteller.

Fliers advertising the event were written in multiple languages and sent home with all students. These included multilingual RSVPs for parents to indicate their plans to attend. Fliers also were posted in apartment buildings in the neighborhood, and phone calls were made prior to the event to remind parents about the Extravaganza.

Arts Extravaganza Family Night provided a venue to promote the arts and artistic expression and to encourage families to share their experiences at home and in their communities. Highwood Hills is building a positive school climate where its students' cultures are respected and celebrated.

Source: Adapted from Highwood Hills Elementary School, in J. I. Brownstein et al., *Promising Partnership Practices 2006* (Baltimore: National Network of Partnership Schools at Johns Hopkins University, 2006), page 55. Explore this and other ideas at www.partnershipschools.org in the section Success Stories.

You Try It!

Your planning committee may elect to conduct an *Arts Extravaganza Family Night* that spotlights the arts of many nations and that increases the involvement of diverse families in your school. Here are a few things to consider.

Identify Artistic Skills and Talents. There is a great deal of hidden talent in every school. Start by talking with teachers and staff about an *Arts Extravaganza Family Night*. List how they can help and their ideas for reaching out to parents of students from many nations. Gather students' ideas. Some students will reveal their own talent or nominate a parent, sibling, or relative with artistic talent. Survey parents in informal interviews, newsletter tear-offs, e-mail, or on the school's website for volunteers to share multicultural arts, crafts, music, and food at the *Extravaganza*. Outline other things your planning team needs for a successful event and ask students, teachers, families, and the community to help in ways that match their skills, talents, interests, and time.

Identify Cultures to Feature. Highwood Hills Elementary School featured arts, crafts, and music from the cultures and countries of its students and families. In schools with less diversity, an *Arts Extravaganza Family Night* might highlight the arts of countries that students study in class. If there are many cultures and artistic volunteers, the planning committee may select different countries each year.

Evaluate Results. An *Arts Extravaganza Family Night* aims to promote multicultural awareness and appreciation of the arts of different cultures and to give students opportunities for artistic expression. It is important to learn whether these goals were met by using exit evaluations of attendees, discussions with teachers and students, and reflective evaluations by the planning committee. An exit evaluation (pages 140–141) gives feedback to the planning committee and ideas for improvement. An evaluation by the planning committee (page 142) assesses the quality of teamwork, support, outreach, and results of the activity and ideas for improvement (Epstein et al., 2009).

Collaborate with the Community. Identify business partners who will support *Arts Extravaganza Family Night* with food, supplies, door prizes, and art materials. There may be artists, musicians, and other volunteers in your community who represent the students' countries of origin or cultures of interest. Ethnic newspapers, radio, TV stations, and civic organizations may provide information to parents and encourage their attendance. A local museum or cultural group may have art or artifacts to share from the selected countries. The public library (and school library) may have age-appropriate books and book lists that give more information about the countries featured at the *Arts Extravaganza Family Night*.

A Different Design Tiempos Felices: Arte, Danza, Música (Happy Times: Art, Dance, Music)

Arts Extravaganza Family Night at Highwood Hills featured the arts of many nations. It was conducted in one large area. Students and family members selected different stations to learn about the arts and crafts from the countries of origin of students' families.

There are other ways to explore the world through the arts. The variation *Tiempos Felices* illustrates how a school can focus on one culture, using three art forms and multiple sites in the school. Attendees move from one place to the next to experience three different Latino arts activities.

Purpose

Tiempos Felices introduces students and their families to literature, art, and dance in the Latino culture. The event not only celebrates the arts, but also enables parents to meet each other, talk with teachers, and experience the school's appreciation for the Latino culture. Schools may adapt this design to spotlight a different cultural group or a country that students study.

Participants are divided into thirds or into groups of twenty people (parents and students). As they sign in, each family is given a folder marked with a red, blue, or green dot.

A chart such as the following should be in each folder to show each group's schedule of activities.

Group	5:00–5:30*	5:30–6:00	6:00–6:30	6:30–7:00
Group 1 – red	Cafeteria *(all groups begin with dinner)*	Library *(literature)*	Classroom *(art)*	Gym *(dance)*
Group 2 – blue		Gym *(dance)*	Library *(literature)*	Classroom *(art)*
Group 3 – green		Classroom *(art)*	Gym *(dance)*	Library *(literature)*

*This schedule allocates twenty-five minutes for each session with five minutes to travel from one place to the next. Time periods may be adjusted for the school and population. Large groups will require duplicate sessions to limit group size to about twenty parents and students.

Planning

1. Prior to *Tiempos Felices*, the planning committee may identify one or more restaurants or ethnic organizations in the community that will donate the dinner for the evening. Alternatively, other arrangements must be made to purchase dinner or to organize potluck suppers for the number of students, family members, and teachers who register for the event. This should be a Latino-inspired dinner such as tacos or burritos. Tortilla chips and salsa, guacamole, rice pudding, and flan custard may be served.

2. Prepare all materials for the dinnertime activity. If a class or grade level will present a story or dance, select the group and schedule time to prepare and rehearse.

3. This event is appropriate for elementary grades. It may be adapted for the middle grades by placing more responsibility for activities on the students and by selecting an age-appropriate book for the library session.

Activity (30 minutes)

1. All attendees will convene in the cafeteria for a light dinner.

2. Play Latin music quietly during dinner.

3. Post a map of the world with Latino countries labeled and highlighted.

4. The principal will give greetings in English and in Spanish (with an interpreter, if needed) to welcome families and explain the purpose and organization of *Tiempos Felices*.

5. One class or grade level may present artwork, a story or play, or a dance that students learned about the Latino culture (optional).

6. Give the red, blue, and green groups directions to the first activity on their schedules.

Concurrent Session: Literature (Library)

Purpose

The library group leader will read aloud *I Love Saturdays y domingos* by Alma Flor Ada. This book, available in English and in Spanish, is recommended as an authentic and culturally sensitive book to read aloud with students. It leads to a discussion of cultural differences and similarities between the main character's maternal and paternal grandparents.

Materials

All materials should be translated, as needed.

- *I Love Saturdays y domingos* by Alma Flor Ada
- A recommended reading list of culturally authentic Latino children's books, by grade level (prepared by the public or school librarian)
- Applications for a public library card

Planning

1. Choose a leader for this session who speaks English and Spanish.

2. Prior to the event, get copies of *I Love Saturdays y domingos* by Alma Flor Ada in English and in Spanish.

3. Prepare a display of books on Latino (and other multicultural) themes for students at different grade levels from the school or public library.

4. Ask the school librarian or public librarian to prepare reading lists of culturally authentic children's books, arranged by grade level, to distribute to parents. Have ready applications for public library cards.

5. Provide a handout for parents on the *Colorin Colorado* website. *Colorin Colorado* is a free, bilingual website for parents and educators that aims to encourage students to read for pleasure. It includes recommended reading lists for students at different age levels. Visit www.colorincolorado.org/read/forkids/recommended?startnum=21.

6. Leaders may select other books to match students' interests, family backgrounds, or themes of family nights.

Activity

1. Introduce the book *I Love Saturdays y domingos* by Alma Flor Ada. Explain that this story is about a bilingual girl who spends weekends with her two sets of English-speaking and Spanish-speaking grandparents.

2. Before reading, discuss character development as a major component of a story.

   Explain: Every story has important parts. Tonight we will talk about *character development*. Let's talk about the characters in stories that you know.

   - When you read a story, what do you want to know about the characters?
   - Why is character development important in a story?
   - How can we learn about different cultures in stories from the experiences of the main character?

3. Tell students and families that in this story, a young girl visits her English-speaking Grandma and Grandpa on Saturdays and her Spanish-speaking *Abuelita* (Grandmother) and *Abuelito* (Grandfather) on *domingos* (Sundays).

4. Read the book to the group. As you read, point out the illustrations and comment on some of the different experiences the main character has with her grandparents.

5. Discuss the story with the students and families:

    ◆ Did you like the story? Why or why not?
    ◆ Who are the main characters?
    ◆ How are the girl's experiences with her two sets of grandparents similar? How are they different?
    ◆ What did you learn about the cultures of the two sets of grandparents from this story?

6. Ask families to talk together about what students like to do best with a grandparent or another member of the family.

7. Show students and their families a few other books from the school library or public library with multicultural themes.

8. Distribute handouts of the multicultural book list, the *Colorin Colorado* website for parents, and applications for public library cards, as needed.

9. Direct the group to their next activity, according to their color-coded schedule.

Concurrent Session: Art of Mexico (Classroom)

Purpose

Families will share favorite holiday traditions and make traditional Mexican flowers to take home.

Materials

Provide enough of these materials so that all attendees can make at least one flower.

◆ 4 sheets of tissue paper (any color)—6″ x 12″ each
◆ 1 pipe cleaner for each flower
◆ Scissors
◆ Ruler
◆ Coloring marker (optional)
◆ Perfume (optional)
◆ One bag per family to carry flowers home
◆ *The History of Mexican Tissue Flowers* (pages 34–35, English and Spanish)
◆ *How to Make a Mexican Tissue Flower* (pages 36–37, English and Spanish)

Planning

1. Prepare a display to show the steps for making one flower.

2. Prepare handout for each family: *The History of Mexican Tissue Flowers*.

3. Prepare handout of *How to Make a Mexican Tissue Flower*.

4. Mexican music, to play quietly as background (optional)

Activity

1. Explain that *fiestas* (or holidays) in Mexico are, indeed, very festive. Bright colors and pretty decorations, including paper flowers, piñatas, colorful blankets, and paper weaving, often set the mood.

2. Discuss how all families have holiday traditions.

   Ask: What do you do in your family to make one of your holidays festive and fun?

   Give families time to talk together about their own holiday traditions and customs. Then, ask one or two to share their ideas with the whole group.

3. Distribute handouts on *The History of Mexican Tissue Flowers* and *How to Make a Mexican Tissue Flower*.

4. Explain that everyone will make at least one Mexican tissue flower to take home. Use the display and sample flower that was prepared to show the steps. The students and families can work along step by step.

5. If there is extra time and available materials, the students and families may make additional flowers.

6. Give each family a bag to carry their flowers home.

7. Direct the group to their next activity, according to their color-coded schedule.

The History of Mexican Tissue Flowers

There is a long tradition in Mexico of constructing flowers using colored tissue paper. It started more than 200 years ago and continues to this day.

Origins of Mexican Paper Crafting

Paper crafting came across the Pacific Ocean from the Philippines to Mexico. Sometimes, tissue paper is called *papel de China* (paper from China) or *papel de seda* (paper of silk). Mexican artists make many things from paper, including *piñatas* (animal figures made of paper and filled with treats) and beautiful paper flowers.

Paper flowers became popular in colonial times (before the 1800s) when Spain ruled Mexico. Originally, the paper flowers were smaller and less colorful than those found today. Most were white or cream colored.

Paper flowers were used in churches and homes. When candles began being used in churches, paper flowers were barred because they posed a fire hazard. Over time, paper flowers became more secular (less religious), more elegant, and more colorful.

Artisans and Their Craft

As paper crafting became popular, artists began to create many kinds of flowers—such as roses, carnations, and zinnias. Some artists copy nature and make twelve (or more) varieties of flowers. Some artists pass their skills along to their children, from generation to generation.

Today, paper flowers are used to decorate homes, fairs, altars, graves, and many other places. In some regions of Mexico, people decorate cakes with paper flowers. Tourists in Mexico may find handcrafted paper flowers in hotel rooms. They also are sold in stores and from stands on the street.

Why Tissue Paper?

Tissue paper is not expensive, compared to real flowers, which can be costly. Tissue paper flowers last a long time.

Source: Adapted from R. A. Garcia at www.ehow.com/print/about_5368006_history-mexican-tissue-flowers.html.

La Historia de las Flores de Papel de China

Hay una tradición en México de hacer flores usando papel de China de colores desde hace mucho tiempo. Empezó hace más de 200 años y sigue hasta hoy.

Los Orígenes de la Artesanía de Papel Mexicana

La artesanía de papel vino de las islas Filipinas a México cruzando el Océano Pacífico. A veces al papel se le llama *papel de China o papel de seda.* Los artistas mexicanos hacen muchas cosas con el papel incluso *piñatas* (formas de animales hechos de papel y rellenos de dulces) y flores bellas.

Las flores de papel se hicieron populares en la época colonial (antes de los años 1800s) cuando México estuvo bajo el dominio de España. Originalmente, las flores de papel eran más pequeñas y de menos color que las flores de hoy. La mayoría eran de color blanco o crema.

Las flores de papel se usaban en las iglesias y en los hogares. Cuando en las iglesias se empezó a usar velas, el uso de las flores de papel se prohibió por riesgos de incendio. Luego, las flores de papel se hicieron más seculares (menos religiosas), elegantes, y llenas de color.

Los Artesanos y su Arte

A medida que la artesanía de papel se hizo más popular, los artistas empezaron a crear muchas clases de flores—como rosas y claveles. Algunos artistas hacen doce (o más) variedades de flores copiando a la naturaleza. Algunos artistas pasan sus habilidades a sus hijos, de generación a generación.

Hoy, las flores de papel se usan para decorar hogares, ferias, altares, tumbas, y muchos otros lugares. En algunas regiones de México, la gente decora pasteles con flores de papel. Los turistas en México pueden encontrar flores de papel hechas a mano en sus cuartos de hoteles. También, estas flores se venden en las tiendas y en los puestos en la calle.

¿Por qué Papel de China?

Papel de China no es caro, a comparación de las flores reales, que pueden ser costosas. Las flores de papel de China duran mucho tiempo.

Fuente: Recuperado y adaptado de R. A. Garcia en www.ehow.com/print/about_5368006_history-mexican-tissue-flowers.html.

How to Make a Mexican Tissue Flower

1. Stack 4 pieces of tissue paper together.	
2. Holding the paper longways, fold the tissue papers together starting at the bottom (like a fan). Fan-fold back and forth making 1 inch folds—about six times.	
3. Cut the folded tissue at both ends as shown, rounding off the corners.	
4. Fold a pipe cleaner in half. Squeeze the tissue paper in the middle and twist the pipe cleaner tightly to secure the folded papers together. The pipe cleaner also serves as the stem of the flower.	
5. Fan out the tissue paper on both sides of the pipe cleaner. Remember there are 4 layers. Gently pull up the petals. Start with the top tissue, being careful not to tear it. After the top layer, go on to the second layer, then the third and the fourth. Straighten out the flower to your liking. Trim the layers of tissue to your liking.	
6. If you wish, use a marker to add more color to your flower.	
7. Shape one side of the pipe cleaner to look like a leaf. Or twist the pipe cleaner to make a thick stem. If you wish, spray a mist of perfume on the flower.	

Source: Retrieved and adapted from www.kckpl.lib.ks.us/ys/CRAFTS/papflowr.htm.

Cómo Hacer una Flor de Papel China Mexicana

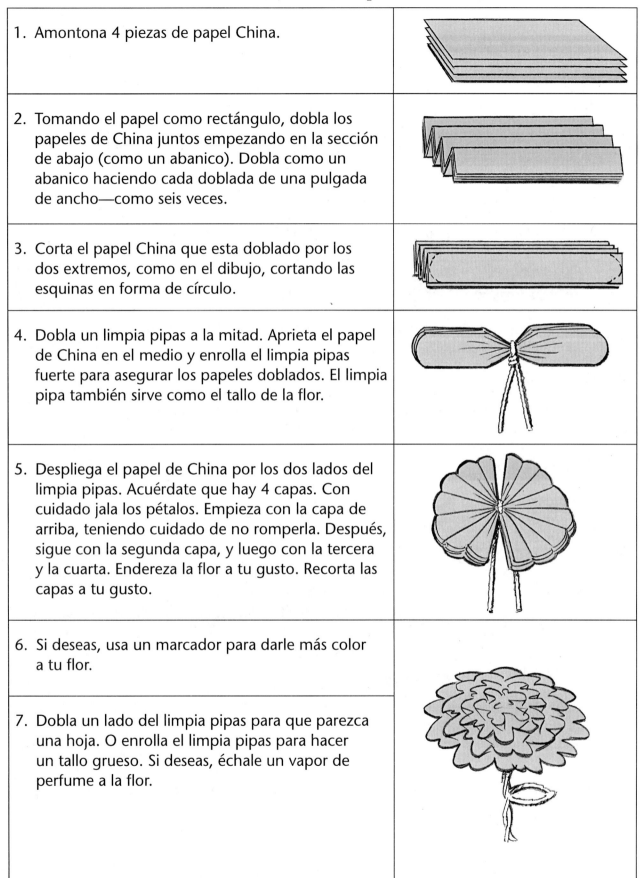

1. Amontona 4 piezas de papel China.

2. Tomando el papel como rectángulo, dobla los papeles de China juntos empezando en la sección de abajo (como un abanico). Dobla como un abanico haciendo cada doblada de una pulgada de ancho—como seis veces.

3. Corta el papel China que esta doblado por los dos extremos, como en el dibujo, cortando las esquinas en forma de círculo.

4. Dobla un limpia pipas a la mitad. Aprieta el papel de China en el medio y enrolla el limpia pipas fuerte para asegurar los papeles doblados. El limpia pipa también sirve como el tallo de la flor.

5. Despliega el papel de China por los dos lados del limpia pipas. Acuérdate que hay 4 capas. Con cuidado jala los pétalos. Empieza con la capa de arriba, teniendo cuidado de no romperla. Después, sigue con la segunda capa, y luego con la tercera y la cuarta. Endereza la flor a tu gusto. Recorta las capas a tu gusto.

6. Si deseas, usa un marcador para darle más color a tu flor.

7. Dobla un lado del limpia pipas para que parezca una hoja. O enrolla el limpia pipas para hacer un tallo grueso. Si deseas, échale un vapor de perfume a la flor.

Fuente: Recuperado y adaptado de www.kckpl.lib.ks.us/ys/CRAFTS/papflowr.htm.

Concurrent Session: Salsa Dance (Gym)

Purpose

Students and families will identify Latin American countries on a map and learn to salsa dance.

Materials

- Latin American salsa music, player, and AV system, if needed.
- *Salsa Dancing* (pages 40–41, English and Spanish).
- Map of the world with Latin American countries labeled and highlighted.

Planning

1. Prepare handouts for all families: *Salsa Dancing* (history and steps).

2. Identify someone to demonstrate salsa dancing. This may be a gym teacher or a family or community volunteer.

Activity

1. Play Latin music softly in the gym as students and families gather.

2. Introduce the activity with a short discussion of how music helps us understand a culture.

    Ask:
    - Do you like to dance?
    - What dances do you do?
    - When do you dance—on what occasions?

3. **Explain:** Today we are going to learn to salsa dance. Salsa is a popular dance style in Latin America that also is popular in the United States and around the world. (Refer to the map posted in the gym that highlights Latin American countries.) Many dance steps that originated in Latin America can be used to salsa dance. We will learn one of them today.

4. Distribute the handout.

5. The dance leader and a partner will describe and demonstrate the steps, following the guidelines in the handout.

   ◆ First, demonstrate the steps without music.
   ◆ Then, demonstrate the steps with music.
   ◆ Then, have the students and families practice individually, without music.
   ◆ Next, have them practice with a partner, without music (to learn the steps, it is OK for girls to dance with girls, boys with mom or dad).
   ◆ Finally, have partners practice with music. Enjoy!

6. Direct the group to their next activity, according to their color-coded schedule.

Bonus Activity (Gym)

Foto Fiesta! In one corner of the gym, set up a spot for family pictures. Those who completed Mexican flowers can include them in the picture. Sombreros, serapes, and pre-made Mexican flowers may be available in the area for families to add to their photos.

Salsa Dancing

Salsa means *sauce* in Spanish. It suggests something "spicy" in Latin American and Caribbean cuisine and in dancing. Latin rhythms from Cuba, Puerto Rico, Mexico, and many other locations are popular in salsa dancing. Our dance lesson today draws from the dance called the mambo, but steps for the Cuban rumba and cha-cha also fit the salsa rhythm. Dancers are encouraged to make up their own steps to the music.

These dances have been popular in Latin America and around the world for many years. The term *salsa dancing* was introduced in the 1970s—perhaps to spice up interest in Latin music and dance.

Basic Salsa Step Diagram (Male or Partner 1)
- The numbers (1, 2, 3...) count the BEAT of the music.
- The gray foot shows where Partner 1's weight is on that BEAT.
- A "break" means stepping forward and then rocking back.
- Have fun!

Salsa Dancing

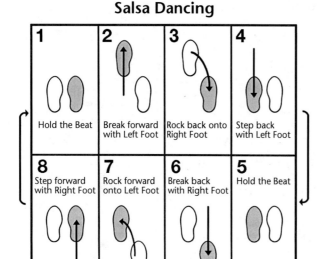

Basic Salsa Step (Female or Partner 2)
- In dance position, partners face each other.
- Partner 2 mirrors the steps of Partner 1.
- When Partner 1 goes forward, Partner 2 goes backward, and so on.

Partner 2 starts with both feet together.
1. Hold the beat.
2. Step BACK with the RIGHT foot.
3. Rock FORWARD onto LEFT foot.
4. Step FORWARD with RIGHT foot.
5. Hold the Beat.
6. Step FORWARD with LEFT foot.
7. Rock BACK onto RIGHT foot.
8. Step BACK with LEFT foot.
9. Repeat, starting at Step 1.

Source: Retrieved and adapted from www.justsalsa.com.

Bailando Salsa

Salsa significa *salsa* en Español. En la cocina y baile Latinoamericano y Caribeño sugiere algo "picante". Los ritmos Latinos de Cuba, Puerto Rico, México, y de otros lugares son populares en la salsa. Nuestra lección de baile de hoy saca del baile llamado mambo, pero pasos de la rumba Cubana y el chacha también encajan con el ritmo de la salsa. Los bailadores son animados a inventar sus propios pasos de música.

Estos bailes han sido populares en Latinoamérica y en otras partes del mundo por muchos años. El termino *salsa* fue introducido en los años 1970s—quizá para aumentar el interés por la música y el baile Latino.

Diagrama del Paso Básico de la Salsa (Hombre o Pareja 1)
- Los números (1, 2, 3…) cuentan el RITMO de la música.
- El pie gris muestra donde el peso de la Pareja 1 está en ese RITMO.
- Una "quebrada" significa dar un paso adelante y luego balanceando atrás.
- ¡Diviértete!

Bailando Salsa

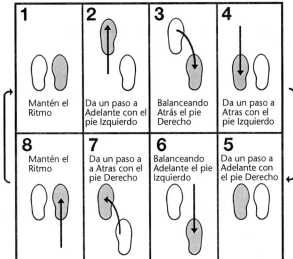

Paso Básico de la Salsa (Mujer o Pareja 2)
- En posición de bailar, las parejas están uno frente al otro.
- La Pareja 2 refleja los pasos de la Pareja 1.
- Cuando la Pareja 1 va adelante, la Pareja 2 va hacia atrás, y así continúan.

La Pareja 2 empieza con ambos pies juntos.
1. Mantén el ritmo.
2. Da un paso a ATRAS con el pie DERECHO.
3. Balanceando ADELANTE el pie IZQUIERDO.
4. Da un paso a ADELANTE con el pie DERECHO.
5. Mantén el ritmo.
6. Da un paso a ADELANTE con el pie IZQUIERDO.
7. Balanceando ATRAS el pie DERECHO.
8. Da un paso a ATRAS con el pie IZQUIERDO.
9. Repite, empezando con el número 1.

Fuente: Recuperado y adaptado de www.justsalsa.com.

CHAPTER 4
Games People Play

Children around the world play many sports and games. As children play, they also learn. When students and their families play games together, they all gain from the shared experience. The following activity shows how one school organized an international games night to help students, families, and teachers learn something new about other countries and have fun at the same time.

Featured Activity Games from Around the World

In Pasco, Washington, an evening of board games for students and parents took on an international and educational twist at Ruth Livingston Elementary School's *Games from Around the World*. The idea came from two Livingston students who entered Pasco School District's annual Family Involvement Essay Contest. In the contest that year, district leaders for partnerships invited students to invent an activity that would bring their parents to the school and increase positive connections between home and school. The two grand prize–winning students from Livingston wrote that they wanted an Around the World Night and a Family Board Game Night. Combining the two, school administrators proposed an international family board game event. The school received $500 in prize money from the district to implement the students' combined activity.

The first task on the to-do list was to identify and purchase about twenty-five games from around the world, including Jenga, jacks, hopscotch, Chinese Checkers, and Mancala. The games were displayed in the school's library to generate excitement and to advertise the game night.

Volunteers greeted the participants at the door and gave each family member a passport and a world map. The map spotlighted the location of the eight countries from which the evening's games originated, with pictures of their national flags and the featured games. The maps also included a series of "fun facts" about the games. About 250 parents and children participated.

Parent-child teams made their way around the gymnasium, stopping at game stations to shoot marbles, jump rope, and play other games, all the while learning new and interesting information about different cultures. As students completed games at each station, they received a passport stamp signifying that they had visited that "country."

Every student who attended *Games from Around the World* entered a raffle for a chance to win one of the games from the event. As a bonus at the end of the activity, a teacher and a student from the local high school invited families to have their photos taken together.

School staff and families enjoyed the combination of fun and learning. Community support helped to keep the price of the event low. A local craft business created and donated the passports and Toys R Us discounted the cost of the games. In total, *Games from Around the World* cost Livingston Elementary about $350.

Source: Adapted from Ruth Livingston Elementary School, in D. J. Hutchins, *Promising Partnership Practices 2008* (Baltimore: National Network of Partnership Schools at Johns Hopkins University, 2008), page 58. Explore this and other ideas at www.partnershipschools.org in the section Success Stories.

You Try It!

Your school's planning committee may elect to conduct *Games from Around the World* to spotlight games from different countries. If you conduct this activity, here are a few things to consider.

Increase Students' Ownership. Pasco School District conducts an annual essay contest for students to submit ideas on ways to increase the involvement of all families. The district serves mainly Latino students and families in economically stressed neighborhoods. The district and its schools strive to involve mothers and fathers in ways that support student achievement and success. At Livingston Elementary, one student's essay suggested that an evening of games for students, parents, and teachers would improve the school climate and help more families feel comfortable about coming to the school and talking with teachers. An important feature of the essay contest was that the district provided a $500 award for each school to implement a winning activity. This showed, clearly, that students' ideas are valued.

Purchase Games. The district's award to the school for its winning essay paid for the twenty-five games that were used in *Games from Around the World*. Toys R Us discounted the price of the games for the school. You may find a community partner to support your school's activity, especially if you can show that the event is part of a larger, ongoing effort to engage all families in their children's education in ways that contribute to student success.

Design a Fun and Learning Night. At Livingston, about 250 people attended this event. The large turnout could be due to the school's work, over time, to develop a culture of partnership. It also could be due, in part, to the nature of the event. A night of games is less intimidating for some parents than a formal meeting with teachers. *Games from Around the World* also appealed to students. Students developed the idea and also saw the games displayed at the school. The students wanted to come back to play the games and sold their parents on the idea of attending. The activities were not only fun and games. Students and families gathered information, practiced map skills, and met many new neighbors as they moved from country to country to play the next game. It is well known that when students are actively involved in an activity at school, parents attend in greater numbers. Your school may agree that it is a good idea to start with a friendly, nonthreatening event to strengthen its partnership program. Then, the planning committee and teachers may move on to more academically oriented activities for parental involvement. Even on a fun night, however, there are many ways to include some good learning activities.

A Different Design | International Favorites— Games People Play

Games from Around the World was creatively conceived, well planned, well implemented, and enjoyed by a large number of parents, students, and teachers. It may have included some games from the countries of origin of students' families, but the goal was more general—to help all students learn about games children play around the world.

Everyone has memories of favorite childhood games—ball games, rope games, team games, and more. This alternative example, *International Favorites: Games People Play*, shows how to organize a game night linked to the home countries of students' families. With good planning and a welcoming spirit, parents and other family members (grandparents, aunts, uncles, and others) tap their memories and take active roles to teach their favorite childhood games to students, other families, and teachers at the school. In a school with little international diversity, parents and grandparents still may share and teach games they played as children.

Purpose

In *Games People Play*, parents and other family members and community members show students, families, and teachers how to play sports and games that they enjoyed when they were children in their home countries. To give students time to learn a game and play it for fun, the students and their families sign up for two or three games of their choice.

Materials

- *Games People Play* invitations for parents (pages 48–49, English and Spanish)
- Tables, booths, or classrooms for game locations
- Signs for game locations
- Game equipment and pieces
- Copies of *Game Card* (pages 50–51, English and Spanish)
- Sign-in sheets and exit evaluations for participants (pages 139–141, English and Spanish)

Planning

The planning committee should plan a two-hour game time in the evening or late afternoon.

1. Recruit families to lead their favorite childhood games in one segment of the event. The family and student who teach a game at one time will be free to select games to play in the other two game periods. Distribute *Games People Play* to invite parents and other family members to sign up to teach a game or to indicate that they will attend.

2. Send the invitation home with students, or arrange for parents to respond via an e-list or on the school's website. Collect RSVPs from families who will attend so that the planning committee will have enough food and enough games for everyone.

3. Make personal calls to multicultural families who did not volunteer in order to encourage their participation and to ensure that the home countries of the students' families are represented with a favorite childhood game. If parents are shy about this active role, suggest that they work with another family member, neighbor, or friend from their native land.

4. The planning committee will compile the parents' responses to the invitations to identify the families who will serve as game leaders.

5. Using the number of families who said that they would attend, plan the number of booths and games that will be conducted in two or three game periods at the event. In the planning process, consider the number of people coming, games needed, number of people learning each game in each game period, space per game in a large room (e.g., gym, playground) or in separate classrooms, and tables or equipment needed. The planning committee may find it useful to set up a database to organize this information and to create a "map" of the games that families will teach in each game period, their locations at the school, and the equipment needed.

6. Schedule the games in two to three sessions of at least 30 minutes each. For example, if 20 families agree to teach games in each game period and 120 other families (adults and children) sign up to attend the event, there will be about six learners (two to three families) at each station in each game period.

7. Families who teach games in one session will be free to play games in other time periods. Provide a schedule and locations (booth, table, classroom) to the families teaching a game. The student(s) from the family will assist in teaching the game. Students and families will travel together to learn and play the games they choose.

8. Families teaching a game from their childhood will provide the planning committee with information on the name and rules of the game, the country or city of origin (where they played the game), one fact about that place or about their childhood, and equipment they have or need for the event. The planning committee or other volunteers may prepare a one-page flyer for each game with information on one side and a map of the country or city of origin on the other. More equipment (e.g., balls, ropes, chalk) may be needed as the planning committee considers how many people will learn and play the game in a thirty-minute period.

9. If classrooms are used, they should be clearly marked for the games in each time period. This will make it easy for families to find the games they signed up to play. Movement from one game to the next will be easy and safe.

10. The planning committee should put active team sports for many players on the school field or in a gym (e.g., soccer/football game; full rope jumping).

11. The planning committee may create an overflow space for a large group game or team sport, or a classroom of extra board games for families and students who did not sign up ahead of time.

12. Prepare the *Game Cards* for students and parents to discuss at their tables during the dinner or snack time. Make the number of copies needed for each table.

Resources for Planning Committee

It is interesting that the same games have different names across cultures. See, for example, http://www.topics-mag.com/internatl/traditional_games/section.htm and http://library.thinkquest.org/J0110166/.

Activity

Before the Game (30 minutes)

1 Families will sign in when they arrive and select one game to learn in each game period that is scheduled. Each game may set a limit on how many participants may sign in, based on space and equipment. The sign-in sheets will be posted at the entrance to each game so that game leaders can check attendance and game players know where to go for each time period.

2. If this is an evening event, plan to serve a light dinner or refreshments before the first game period. If *Games People Play* is conducted right after school, plan to serve snacks. While families are eating, they may discuss the *Game Card* placed on each table.

3. The principal and the chair of the planning committee will welcome families, explain the purpose and organization of the evening, and, at the right time, direct the families who are teaching their favorite childhood games in the first game period to go to their game locations. After a short time, the other students and families will be directed to the games they signed up to learn in game period 1. Students and their family members will travel together.

Let the Games Begin (60–90 minutes)

1. There may be two or three game periods of at least thirty minutes each. For the first ten minutes, the parent-leader will show and teach the childhood game, assisted by the student. Then the other students and families will play the game they learned.

2. A teacher or school staff member (e.g., a secretary or counselor) will be at each game location to assist the teaching family or learning families, as needed.

3. After thirty minutes, a bell or signal will direct families to the next game period. The teaching families will move first to their game location, followed in a few minutes by the others. The sign-in sheets for game period 2 will be posted at the entrance to the games so everyone can find their correct locations.

4. Additional game periods (if scheduled) will follow the same pattern.

Reflections (15 minutes)

At the end of the final game period, bring everyone together in one large space to talk about the games from other countries that parents enjoyed when they were children.

- ◆ What was similar between these games and games today?
- ◆ What was different?

The planning committee may have door prizes to distribute. These may include commercially sold multicultural board games to sustain the theme of the evening. Parents and students should evaluate their experiences at *Games People Play* using the exit evaluation form in the Appendix.

Games People Play: *You Are Invited!*

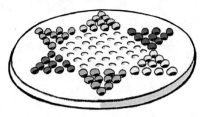

Dear Parent or Family Member:

Games are fun to play and help teach strategic thinking, sharing, and good sportsmanship.

Did you have a favorite childhood game? Would you teach it to others?

We will have a *Games People Play* Family Fun Night on _____.
We invite you and your student(s) to lead one game period (30 minutes) by sharing a favorite childhood game with other students and families. At *Games People Play*, you and your family will have dinner, teach your game in one session, and learn a game in the next session.

Please check below if you will teach a game, if you will attend *Games People Play*, or if you cannot participate this time.

Name of Student_____ Grade Level_____

Name of Parent_____

☐ **YES. My student and I will teach a game.**

Which game from your childhood will you teach?_____
Name of Game

As a child, where did you play this game?_____
Name of Country or City

This game requires the following (describe):

Space or table_____

Equipment_____

The Planning Committee will contact you with information about this activity.

When is the best time to call you?_____ _____
Phone Number   Best Time to Call

☐ **YES. We will attend *Games People Play* (but will not teach a game this time).**

How many from your family will attend? _____ Adults _____ Children

☐ **NO. Sorry, we cannot attend this time.**

Please return this RSVP to_____ by (date)_____

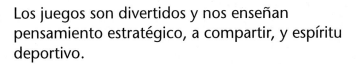

Juegos que la Gente Juega: *¡Está invitado!*

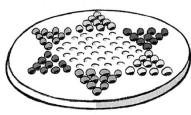

Estimado Padre o Miembro de Familia:

Los juegos son divertidos y nos enseñan pensamiento estratégico, a compartir, y espíritu deportivo.

¿Tuvo un juego favorito de niño? ¿Se lo enseñaría a otros?

Tendremos una Noche Familiar de *Juegos que la Gente Juega* en _____. Le invitamos a usted y a su estudiante(s) a liderar un periodo de juego (30 minutos) y compartir su juego de niño favorito con otros estudiantes y familias. En *Juegos que la Gente Juega*, usted y su familia cenarán, enseñarán su juego en una sesión, y aprenderán un juego en la siguiente sesión.

Por favor indique si desea enseñar un juego, asistir a la Noche Familiar de *Juegos que la Gente Juega*, o si no puede participar.

Nombre del Estudiante_____ Grado_____

Nombre del Padre_____

☐ Sí. Mi estudiante y yo enseñaremos un juego.

¿Cuál juego enseñará?_____
Nombre del Juego

¿Cuando niño, dónde jugó este juego?_____
Nombre del País o Ciudad

Este juego requiere lo siguiente (describa):

Espacio o mesa_____

Artículos/materiales_____

El Comité de Planificación le contactará con información acerca de esta actividad.

¿Cuándo es la mejor hora para llamarle?_____ _____
Numero Telefónico   Mejor Hora para Llamar

☐ Sí. Asistiremos a la Noche Familiar de *Juegos que la Gente Juega* (pero esta vez no enseñaremos un juego).

¿Cuántos miembros de su familia asistirán? _____ Adultos _____ Niños

☐ NO. Lo siento, no podemos asistir esta vez.

Favor de devolver su respuesta a_____ en (la fecha)_____

Games People Play: Game Card

Games are fun to play and help teach strategic thinking, sharing, and good sportsmanship. While we wait for games to begin, discuss your memories and ideas about a favorite game.

Parents and Family Members: Think of a favorite game that you played as a child.
Students: Think of your favorite game this year.

Fill in the chart below and talk about your memories and experiences.

Name of Family Member	Name the Game Adults: Favorite game in childhood? Students: Favorite game now?	Where did/do you play this game?	What equipment did/do you need to play it? What are the rules?	Why did/do you like this game?	What happened if you won the game? What happened if you lost the game?

Discuss: What is good sportsmanlike behavior for the games you listed?

Juegos que la Gente Juega: Tarjeta de Juego

Los juegos son divertidos y nos enseñan pensamiento estratégico, a compartir, y espíritu deportivo. Mientras esperamos que los juegos inicien, comparte tus memorias e ideas sobre un juego favorito.

Padres y Miembros de Familia: Piensen en un juego favorito de su niñez.

Estudiantes: Piensa en tu juego favorito de este año.

Llenen la tarjeta y compartan sus memorias y experiencias.

Nombre del Miembro de Familia	Nombre del Juego **Adultos:** ¿Juego favorito de su niñez? **Estudiantes:** ¿Juego favorito hoy?	¿Dónde jugó/juega este juego?	¿Qué artículos/materiales necesitó/necesita para jugarlo? ¿Cuáles son las reglas?	¿Por qué le gusto/gusta este juego?	¿Qué pasó si ganó el juego? ¿Qué pasó si perdió el juego?

Comparta:¿Cuál es un ejemplo de buen espíritu deportivo de los juegos que anotaron?

CHAPTER 5
A School of Many Nations

All students in a school share the place and its promise. All students, educators, families, and others in the community hope that their schools will be wonderful, welcoming places where all students learn to their full potential. One common strategy to improve the school climate is staging well-planned, goal-linked family nights. When schools serve diverse families, Multicultural Family Nights send two important messages: *This is everyone's school. You are welcome here.*

The following activity shows how one school celebrated the countries of origin of its students' families. The school's partnership team called on families and members of the community to contribute ideas and resources to make this event a success.

Featured Activity Celebration of Nations

All the pomp of a parade and the organization of an international expo went into preparations for Saeger Middle School's *Celebration of Nations* in St. Charles, Missouri. This event brought students, teachers, parents, and the community together to celebrate the variety of backgrounds represented by Saeger's sixth, seventh, and eighth graders and their families. The celebration welcomed all students and families, showcased students' learning, and promoted the school's multicultural efforts—raising awareness, appreciation, and respect for the diverse backgrounds, languages, experiences, and views of its school population.

The evening kicked off when a line of ESL students paraded into the gym, each bearing the flag of a different nation represented at Saeger. Each student greeted the audience, one by one, in his or her native language. After the students marched out of the gym, attendees were treated to performances by members of the local community college, the wider community, and by students and parents from the school.

Irish clog dancers skipped across the gym floor; an African storyteller used his drums to wrap the audience in a tale; a troupe of Hawaiian dancers captured everyone's attention; and groups of students sang songs in various languages. Following the multicultural variety show, attendees explored other areas of the school where students, parents, and teachers had set up cultural exhibitions. In one area, the French teacher and students prepared crêpes for everyone to enjoy. Mexican cuisine donated by local restaurants was served in another area. Homemade delights including baklava and Indian rice were prepared and served by parent volunteers.

Students' posters and displays about their families' home countries or countries studied in school were on show in the halls. Other display tables in the cafeteria featured coins, clothing, photos, souvenirs, and other cultural objects provided by students, families, teachers, and community members. Students demonstrated and taught others traditional games and crafts from their families' countries of origin, including a tae kwon do routine from Korea, Los Ojos de Dios weaving from Mexico, and origami cranes from Japan.

Source: Adapted from Saeger Middle School in D. J. Hutchins, *Promising Partnership Practices 2009* (Baltimore: National Network of Partnership Schools at Johns Hopkins University, 2009), page 54. Explore this and other ideas at www.partnershipschools.org in the section Success Stories.

You Try It!

Your planning committee may elect to conduct a similar celebration of students' home countries, families' countries of origin, or countries explored in social studies. This kind of big event is welcoming and celebratory, but requires strong teamwork and good planning. If your school implements a *Celebration of Nations*, here are a few things to consider.

Draw from the Curriculum. At Saeger Middle School, students take French, Spanish, or World Language courses. There also is an English as a Second Language (ESL) program for immigrant students. ESL and non-ESL students connect in their classes and in the school's Culture Club. Examine your school's programs to identify where diverse cultures, languages, and customs are studied or experienced. Ask the teachers, students, and families in these programs for ideas for your school's *Celebration of Nations*.

Collaborate with the Community. The community contributed to the success of *Celebration of Nations*. All schools have community resources, although some are not as obvious as others. The planning committee can map all community resources within a mile of the school, noting names of businesses and organizations, leaders, phone numbers, and how they may contribute to activities for family and community involvement (Sanders, 2006). For example, local ethnic restaurants may donate foods so participants can sample cuisines from different cultures. Contact the community partners who may assist with each planned activity.

Involve Students, Teachers, and Parents. In Saeger's *Celebration of Nations*, all members of the school community participated. Many teachers and other staff members helped with all aspects of the event. Students welcomed families, created posters and displays about their countries of origin or countries studied in class, and performed in several demonstrations. Families were key in providing native foods and artifacts. Conduct a survey of parents to learn of their interests, skills, talents, and willingness to share in planning and conducting a *Celebration of Nations* in your school by contributing information, food, music, crafts, a dance performance, or artifacts. Broad participation leads to high attendance and positive energy at the event.

Carry Out a Welcoming Strategy from Start to Finish. In schools that serve multicultural families, make sure that the invitations and publicity are in languages that parents can understand. Have translators involved in preparations and have interpreters at the event to assist families, as needed. Translate the exit evaluation form so that all families can give their views. (See sample exit evaluation forms in English and Spanish in the Appendix, pages 140–141.)

Plan Space and Time. A big event can become overwhelming. Advance planning keep things under control. If students, families, or community groups are entertaining, be sure that there is appropriate space, good sound and lighting equipment, and time for attendees to give performers their full attention. There is nothing worse than too-loud music, a faulty microphone, or a rude audience while singers or dancers are sharing their talents. Plan enough time for students and families to enjoy food and visit booths. Ask parents and students to RSVP to an invititation so that the planning committee will know how much food will be needed. Always plan for some extra servings for people who did not RSVP.

Evaluate Quality. It is important to evaluate what worked well and what should be improved in future activities to welcome diverse families to the school. In addition to attendees' exit evaluations, schedule time for the planning committee to debrief with detailed discussions of the location, space, time allotted, quality of the booths, foods, performers, outreach to all families, participation, and other aspects of the evening. (See a sample reflective evaluation for the planning committee to use in the Appendix, page 142.)

Diversify Designs. Some schools conduct the same event each year and work to improve its organization and outreach. Other schools vary the theme and design for Multicultural Family Nights from year to year. Schools not only celebrate all cultures, but also share specific holidays (e.g., Hmong New Year and Cinco de Mayo), fashions from the nations represented by students' families, and other cultural features. See many designs for multicultural celebrations in the annual books of *Promising Partnership Practices* at www.partnershipschools.org in the section Success Stories.

A Different Design Our Community's Place in the World

The *Celebration of Nations* is a whole-school event to welcome all families, highlight the diversity of backgrounds and cultures in a school, and reinforce the school's emphasis on multicultural awareness and the appreciation of all cultures. The alternative example illustrates how a school may explore diversity and cultural richness in the community.

Purpose

Even in a school with few immigrant families and little diversity in family backgrounds, it is important to open the world to students who might otherwise be insulated and isolated. Every community includes groups and individuals who have past and present connections to other countries around the world. *Our Community's Place in the World* spotlights the connections in the school community that could expand and enrich students' experiences, the school's program, and family activities throughout the year.

Materials

◆ Booths, tables, easels, and/or display boards for community groups and individuals

◆ Map for students and parents of the locations of all booths

◆ Map of the world for students to take on their "trip." They will label and highlight the countries they visit as they tour *Our Community's Place in the World.*

◆ *Passport* (pages 58–59, English and Spanish)

◆ Computers in booths or strategic spots that show interesting information on the featured countries

◆ *Invitation for Community Presenters* (page 60)

◆ Community presenters may bring information on their programs and services to distribute to parents.

Planning

1. The planning committee should meet to outline details for conducting *Our Community's Place in the World.* Consider how members of the planning committee will contact members of the community who have interesting and important international connections that will benefit students, families, and teachers at the school. This activity also will help small businesses, agencies, and organizations in the area publicize their services. The win-win results will encourage community participation.

    Most communities have international ties through:

    ◆ Ethnic restaurants and markets, or those that serve or sell internationally inspired foods

    ◆ Sports and games (e.g., karate, tai kwon do, soccer/*futbol*, players on local teams)

    ◆ Business, trade, and goods (e.g., Pier 1, Trader Joe's, Wal-Mart, clothing stores)

    ◆ Ethnic civic, service, and nonprofit organizations in the community

    ◆ Language programs (e.g., foreign language programs in high schools and colleges)

    ◆ Faith leaders (e.g., pastors, faith leaders from different countries)

    ◆ Hospitals and clinics (e.g., doctors and nurses from different countries)

    ◆ Public library (e.g., librarian may bring books with stories about different countries, or tour books, photograph books, or other references, along with applications for library cards)

    ◆ Alumni from the school who have had international occupations, vacations, or other experiences to share

    ◆ Local media serving ethnic and cultural groups

Volunteers may help the planning committee identify the many international connections of interest and importance to the school and to families.

2. Guide the participants to organize a display of their work, their homeland, or their ties to other countries with photos, artifacts, crafts, or other features that will be of interest to students and their families. Each community partner should include one hands-on activity for students to complete on their visit, such as examining a photo display for particular features, playing a game, or learning a song or dance. When students complete the activity, their passports will be stamped to document their learning experiences.

3. The planning committee should consider the following organizational issues. A committee leader or subgroup may be helpful for planning the event.

   ◆ Timing. Plan two or three hours for students and families to visit, tour, and enjoy *Our Community's Place in the World*.
   ◆ Publicity. Invite the local media to report on the event.
   ◆ Location. Identify a location for each community participant (e.g., a spot in the gym, a particular classroom).
   ◆ Refreshments. After invitations are sent and returned by families indicating the number of people who plan to attend *Our Community's Place in the World*, the planning committee should work with community groups in the food industry to plan the kinds and amount of food for the event.
   ◆ Event Management. A subcommittee may be needed to ensure the smooth implementation of the event. This group of leaders will make sure each "country" has a stamp for the students' passports. Someone may take pictures of the different displays for a school bulletin board or for the school website. The group may organize volunteers to help set up and clean up.

Activity

1. Have families sign in. Provide each student with a passport.

2. Give each family a map showing the location of all booths in the cafeteria (or other school location). Students will mark the countries they visit with an X.

3. If entertainment is scheduled, provide each family with a program showing the times and locations of the performances.

4. Provide a meal or light refreshments at the start of the event or have food-linked booths provide snacks throughout the evening.

5. Ask the principal and chair of the planning committee to welcome everyone, thank the community partners, and briefly explain the purpose of *Our Community's Place in the World*.

6. Give ample time for students and their families to travel to visit the community's international activities. Students will complete one hands-on activity at five or more locations and have their passports stamped at each place. They will submit the stamped passports at the end of the event for a drawing for a thematically appropriate prize, such as a globe or atlas.

7. Bring everyone back together at the end of the event for a fifteen-minute reflection activity. Ask students and parents to share one new fact they learned when they visited a particular country.

8. Ask families and students to complete an exit evaluation specifying their reactions and suggestions (pages 140–141).

Our Community's Place in the World: Passport

Student's Name_____

Class/Teachers_____

You and your family are about to travel around the world to visit many countries. At each stop:

    ◆ Mark the country on your map of the world.

    ◆ Complete one activity in each country to learn something new.

    ◆ Then, get your passport stamped.

Try to visit at least five countries. Have a good trip!

Name of Country	Official Stamp	One Thing I Learned...
1.		
2.		
3.		
4.		
5.		
6.		

Use the back of this page if you visit more countries and complete activities.

Submit your passport to enter our international raffle.

El Lugar de Nuestra Comunidad en el Mundo: Pasaporte

Nombre del Estudiante_____

Clase/Maestro(a)_____

Tú y tu familia están a punto de viajar alrededor del mundo para visitar muchos países. En cada parada:

- ◆ Marca el país en tu mapa del mundo.

- ◆ Completa una actividad en cada país para aprender algo nuevo.

- ◆ Después, obtén un sello en tu pasaporte.

Intenta visitar mínimo cinco países. ¡Ten un buen viaje!

Nombre del País	Sello Oficial	Algo que aprendí...
1.		
2.		
3.		
4.		
5.		
6.		

Usa la parte de atrás de esta página si visitas más países y completas actividades.

Entrega tu pasaporte para entrar a nuestra rifa internacional.

Invitation for Community Presenters

(Date)

Dear (Name of Community Partner):

(Name of School) is conducting an important and exciting family night—**Our Community's Place in the World**—on (date). The purpose of this activity is to welcome all families to our school and to help them learn more about the many resources, services, and programs in our community.

You are invited to participate in this activity to share information on your organization's services with our families.

I will follow up with a phone call in a few days to give you specific information about the activity and how you may be involved.

Thank you for considering participation. I hope that you will be able to share your resources and expertise with our students and their families.

Sincerely,

(Name)

(Position)

PART THREE

Workshops for Parents

Workshops for Parents give family members opportunities to meet and share ideas with others, gather ideas, and discuss important topics for their children's development and success in school.

What people are saying:

After *Celebrating Our Differences*, the El Rancho community of students, parents, and staff grew closer together in working towards the goal of improving student achievement. The parents felt welcomed and engaged in their children's education through this and other activities. There was a sign at the school in Spanish and English that said to the parents, "You have a role and a voice at El Rancho Elementary!" This sentiment captures exactly the spirit of this activity.

Carol Garman, Title I/ELD Program Specialist and Leader for Partnerships
Chino Valley Unified School District, California

Chapter 6: Gather Ideas at a Forum

- ◆ *Celebrate Our Differences*, at El Rancho Elementary School, in Chino, California (subsequently consolidated with another school), enabled parents and teachers to communicate, despite their language differences.

- ◆ *Welcome One and All* is an alternative design that shows how to organize a forum that helps parents expand their social networks, improves communications between educators and multicultural families, and results in specific ideas that teachers and parents may implement to create a more welcoming school climate for all.

Chapter 7: Series of Workshops

♦ *International Parent Workshops* from Patterson High School in Baltimore, Maryland, describes monthly meetings that welcome parents new to the school from many countries, smooth their transition to the school, and increase their involvement at the school and in their children's education.

♦ *Grow a Tree of Knowledge* is an alternative design that outlines how to organize a short series of three workshops to help new immigrant parents and others who have been uninvolved in the past become acquainted with the policies and procedures of their child's school.

Chapter 8: Promote Learning at Home

♦ *Opening Windows to Writing* describes how parents at Ranch View Elementary School in Naperville, Illinois, became students for a night and got better acquainted with how their youngsters learn to write.

♦ *Positive Homework Policies and Practices* is an alternative design that shows how any school can conduct a workshop for parents on the school's homework policies and provide positive strategies for parents to support their children at home.

CHAPTER 6 ———————————————
Gather Ideas at a Forum

It is essential to establish positive two-way communications in programs of school, family, and community partnerships. There are countless reasons and many methods to communicate from school to home and from home to school. This chapter shows how well-designed workshops for parents help communications flow to and from more and different parents. Some workshops are designed as forums to share information with parents, gather ideas from parents, and enable parents and educators to discuss topics that are important for students' education and school improvement.

Forums pose some challenges in schools that serve students and families with diverse cultural and linguistic backgrounds. The following activity shows how one elementary school conducted a forum that promoted positive communications with all families, including its large population of Latino parents.

Featured Activity Celebrate Our Differences

El Rancho Elementary School, located in Chino, California, served a large number of Latino students and their families, along with Anglo and other racial and ethnic groups. Before the school closed due to consolidation in 2009, the Action Team for Partnership (ATP) wanted to open lines of communication between parents and teachers and create a more welcoming climate by dispelling cultural misconceptions and stereotypes. The ATP planned *Celebrate Our Differences*, an activity that encouraged parents and teachers to communicate, despite language differences.

The two-hour forum began with a quick icebreaker that enabled parents to meet each other. A school administrator divided about seventy-five parents into small groups, each with at least one teacher representative. Each group received a poster-size sticky note pad, felt pens, and a series of questions about their children's education, such as:

> What are specific ways parents can show their children that they care about their education?
> *¿Cuáles son las formas específicas los padres pueden mostrar sus hijos que cuidado sobre su educación?*

> How can we build a communication bridge between educators and parents at this school?
> *¿Cómo podemos construir un puente de comunicación entre educadores y padres en esta escuela?*

For the next hour, small groups of parents and teachers discussed the questions and wrote their responses in English or in Spanish. After reporting their main ideas to the whole group, a staff member summarized the general findings.

The twist of this forum was that the general presentation was conducted in Spanish, while English-speaking attendees listened to an interpreter through special headsets. Many of the English-speaking parents commented that it was enlightening to experience what the Spanish-speaking parents deal with on a regular basis.

The school's Latino families mentioned that after attending *Celebrate Our Differences*, they felt much more welcome in the building. This forum helped El Rancho build important cultural bridges between school and home.

Source: Adapted from El Rancho Elementary School, in D. J. Hutchins et al., *Promising Partnership Practices 2008* (Baltimore: National Network of Partnership Schools at Johns Hopkins University, 2008), page 57. Explore this and other ideas at www.partnershipschools.org in the section Success Stories.

You Try It!

Your planning committee may elect to conduct a forum like *Celebrate Our Differences* to hear parents' views on important matters and to give English-speaking parents a chance to experience translations in the same way that Latino parents do at many workshops. Here are a few things to consider.

Advertise. El Rancho Elementary School advertised *Celebrate Our Differences* in the school newsletter, on the school website, through fliers, and in the local newspaper. You also may advertise your school's forum on a local radio, TV, or cable station, including popular ethnic or foreign language stations, and in churches, meeting houses, and community centers used by your schools' families. Some fast-food restaurants allow schools to advertise activities on tray liners. When a major workshop is conducted at school, advertising matters!

Translate. Recruit multilingual parents and other family members (as well as district-level support personnel) to translate flyers, ads, and materials and to serve as interpreters at the forum. This saves funds and gives parents leadership roles for the activity and in the school's partnership program.

Encourage Broad Participation. With support from the school's planning committee, Latino parents volunteered to decorate the multipurpose room for *Celebrate Our Differences*. When parents, other family members, and educators share leadership tasks in planning and conducting a workshop (e.g., translating, decorating, bringing food, obtaining community support), more partners gain ownership of the activity and demonstrate more equal partnerships among teachers, administrators, and parents.

Collaborate with Community Partners. The forum *Celebrate Our Differences* aimed to promote conversations among parents and between parents and teachers. Some forums include community partners to gather their ideas about school improvement and to mobilize additional resources to strengthen the school program, increase family services, and improve student learning. Community members (e.g., business owners, neighbors, religious leaders, YMCA, alumni, ethnic organizations) may be valuable partners with educators and parents in improving student attendance, achievement, behavior, and, in upper grades, organizing internships and part-time employment for high school students.

A Different Design Welcome One and All

The forum *Celebrate Our Differences* gathered parents' ideas on how to increase positive communications between a school and its families. It was an easy and unintimidating way for small groups of parents and teachers to meet and share their ideas using their home languages.

The alternative example, *Welcome One and All*, shows how to organize a forum that helps parents expand their social networks, improves communications between educators and multicultural families, and results in specific ideas that teachers and parents may implement to create a more welcoming school climate for all.

This forum builds on three questions that encourage parents and teachers to (1) listen to and appreciate each other's backgrounds and experiences, (2) recognize current good practices at the school, and (3) feel comfortable about generating a list of ideas for improvement. The structure of this forum may be applied to other questions for school improvement.

Purpose

This forum promotes conversations of parents and educators on ways to create a more welcoming school so that all families feel comfortable at the school and able to talk with teachers and administrators about improving the school climate. The discussion also should help educators understand parents' interests in the school and in their children's education.

Materials

- ◆ 3 pieces of chart paper for each table, each piece labeled with one of the workshop questions for discussion
- ◆ A set of markers for each table
- ◆ *Follow-Up Survey for Parents* (pages 71–72, English and Spanish)

Planning

1. Depending on the number of preregistered participants, identify a classroom, cafeteria, or other multipurpose room to conduct the forum.

2. Prepare three pieces of chart paper for each table, with one of the forum's major questions (A, B, C) at the top of each page. This is easily done with a poster-making machine, if available.

   A. *What makes a welcoming climate?* (List characteristics of welcoming places—not only schools.) Where do you feel "welcome" as soon as you walk in the door? What makes you feel that way?

   B. *How does this school welcome students? parents? others?* What does this school do that is welcoming?

   C. *What could educators, parents, and others do to create a more welcoming climate for ALL parents in this school?* (List specific goals and actions that educators, parents, students, and others could take during the next school year.)

Activity

1. Provide a meal or light refreshments at the start of the forum.

2. Invite the principal and the chair of the planning committee to welcome parents and explain the purpose of the forum.

3. Conduct the icebreaker (*Past and Present: Are Schools Different or the Same?* pages 67–70). Summarize important ideas.

4. Have each table select a table leader, timekeeper, and recorder. The table leader will moderate the discussion and make sure that everyone has an opportunity to speak. The timekeeper will make sure the group sticks to the time available and discusses all three questions. The recorder will write the group's ideas for each question on the chart.

5. Allow participants about ten minutes per question to discuss and record their ideas. Be sure that bilingual parents and staff members are at the tables where their translation and interpreting skills are needed so that English- and non-English-speaking parents can communicate with each other.

6. Give a signal (e.g., bell, chime, drum) to guide the groups to move to each new question after ten minutes. The groups will discuss the three questions for about 30 minutes, with time adjusted to meet the forum's schedule (e.g., use 15 minutes per question if 45 minutes are available for the discussion period). Adjust time as needed (e.g., give more time for Question C to record everyone's ideas).

7. Reserve at least 20 minutes for the whole group to discuss their ideas. Focus most of this time on Question C.

8. The principal or forum leader should summarize "next steps," including how the results from the forum will be used. Thank the attendees for their time, energy, interest, and input, and encourage them to participate with the planning committee on other involvement activities.

9. Send home a *Follow-Up Survey* to parents who were unable to attend *Welcome One and All*. The survey provides a short summary of major results from the forum and allows parents who could not attend to suggest ideas for creating a more welcoming school climate for all families. Some parents cannot attend school workshops or meetings if they work during the school day or have other demands on their time. An excellent partnership program will address this common challenge and find ways to provide information to and gather ideas from those who cannot attend school events (also see Chapter 8). Ask classroom teachers to distribute the surveys to students to take home teachers can then collect the completed surveys and return them to the planning committee. The survey may also be placed with a tear-off in the school newsletter or sent to parents by e-mail.

10. Compile all groups' ideas in a useful summary. The planning committee should report the results of this forum in the school newsletter or on the school's website and share the responses with the full faculty, parent organization, school improvement team, and all families.

11. Select two or three of the suggested actions for which there was high agreement to improve the school climate for all families, including immigrant families and others who were uninvolved in the past. These activities should be added to the planning committee's full schedule of involvement activities for the school year (Epstein et al., 2009).

Icebreaker: Past and Present: Are Schools Different or the Same?

Purpose

This icebreaker asks participants to compare their own school experiences with their children's school programs and experiences. Some parents will have been educated in different countries with different educational systems. Others will have attended schools very similar to their child's schools, but years ago. The memories and contrasts will be of interest and encourage discussions among educators, parents, and others at the forum.

Materials

- Pen or pencil for each participant
- Activity page: *Past and Present: Are Schools Different or the Same?* (pages 69–70, English and Spanish)

Activity

1. Organize seating so that diverse attendees sit at each table. For example, table-hats may note seats for Teacher, Parent, Administrator, and Other Partner at a table for four people. Or, using the registration list for the forum, the planning committee may select other meaningful identifiers (e.g., parents with student in grade_____; parents from_____neighborhood; parents from _____country of origin). In this way, participants will talk and work with some people they do not already know.

   Ask those sitting at each table to introduce themselves and tell where they went to school. Make sure that interpreters are at tables, as needed.

2. Place writing instruments and the activity pages for all participants on the tables.

   Show an enlarged activity page on the wall (or on a slide). Explain that each person will work with a partner. Each one will write ideas on the activity page in his or her own language. All partners will describe and record the following:

   - one memory of their own schooling that is different from their child's school
   - one feature of their child's schooling that is different from the past
   - one common experience or similar feature in their own school and the child's school—past and present

3. After about five minutes, ask a few reporters (e.g., one from each table or three volunteers in all) to share one difference or similarity in their own and their child's school experiences. The workshop leader may collect the activity pages to learn more about the school experiences of students' families.

Past and Present:
Are Schools Different or the Same?

How was the school YOU attended the same or different from THIS school?

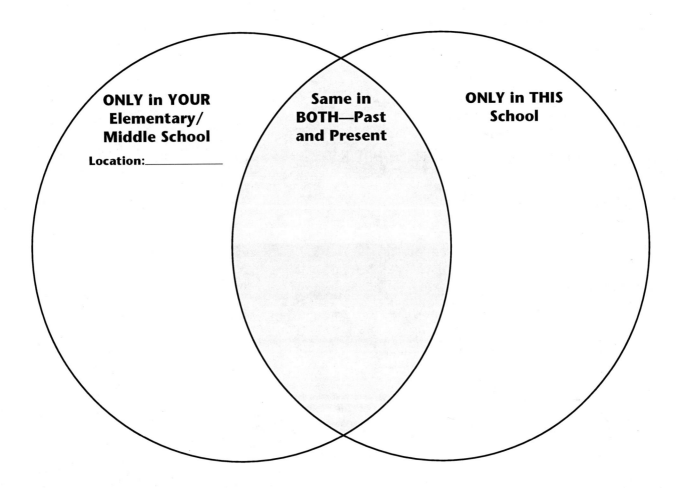

ONLY in YOUR
Elementary/
Middle School

Location:_____

Same in
BOTH—Past
and Present

ONLY in THIS
School

Pasado y Presente:
¿Son las Escuelas Diferentes o Iguales?

¿Cómo era la escuela que TU asististe, igual a o diferente a ESTA escuela?

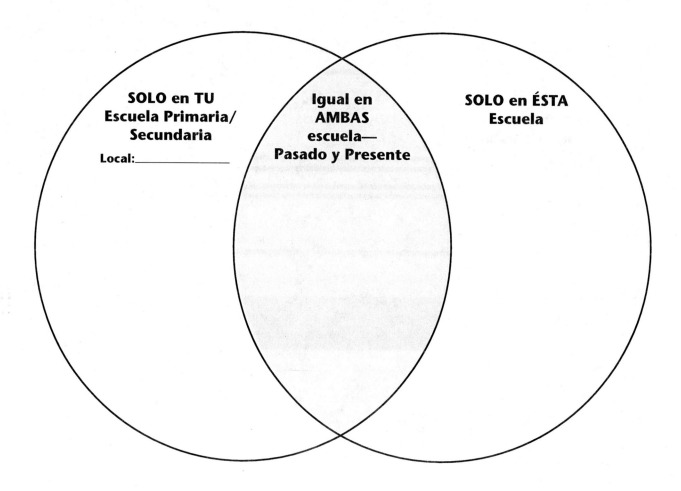

SOLO en TU Escuela Primaria/ Secundaria

Local:_____

Igual en AMBAS escuela— Pasado y Presente

SOLO en ÉSTA Escuela

Follow-Up Survey for Parents

Welcome One and All

Dear Parent or Guardian:

At our school's recent forum, *Welcome One and All*, parents, teachers, and community members shared their views on how to create a more welcoming climate for ALL parents at this school.

Many good ideas were shared at the forum, such as the following (Summarize 2–3 ideas from the forum.):

◆

◆

◆

Unfortunately, some parents were unable to attend, due to conflicting schedules. Here are the questions we discussed. Please share your ideas.

A. What makes a welcoming climate? List one characteristic of a welcoming place you know—not necessarily a school. What makes you feel that way?

One welcoming place I know is: _____

What makes you feel welcome there as soon as you walk in? _____

_____

B. How does this school welcome students? parents?

One good way this school welcomes students is: _____

_____

One good way this school welcomes parents is: _____

_____

C. What do YOU think educators, parents, and others should do to create a *more welcoming climate* in this school for ALL parents?

_____

_____

_____

The planning committee for increasing the involvement of all the school's families will review your ideas and those from the forum. The committee will design and implement two or three activities over the next year to strengthen the school's program of school, family, and community partnerships.

Thank you for your ideas!

Encuesta de Seguimiento para los Padres
Bienvenidos Uno y Todos

Estimado Padre o Tutor:

En el foro de nuestra escuela, *Bienvenidos Uno y Todos*, padres, maestros (as), y miembros de la comunidad compartieron sus opiniones sobre cómo crear un mejor ambiente de bienvenida para TODOS los padres en esta escuela.

Muchas buenas ideas se compartieron en el foro, tales como las siguientes (Resuma 2–3 ideas del foro.):

◆
◆
◆

Desafortunadamente, algunos padres no pudieron asistir, por conflicto de horarios. Aquí están las preguntas que discutimos. Favor de compartir sus ideas.

A. ¿Cuáles son las características de un ambiente donde te sientes bienvenida?
Nombra una característica de un lugar donde te sientas bienvenido—no necesariamente una escuela. ¿Qué es lo que te hace sentir así?

Un lugar donde me siento bienvenido es: _____

¿Qué es lo que le hace sentir bienvenido(a) tan pronto llegas al lugar?_____

_____

B. ¿Cómo esta escuela hace que los estudiantes se sientan bienvenidos? ¿y los padres?

Una buena manera que esta escuela usa para hacer que los estudiantes se sientan bienvenidos es: _____

_____

Una buena manera que ésta escuela usa para hacer que los padres se sientan bienvenidos es:_____

_____

C. ¿Qué es lo que educadores, padres, y otros deberían hacer para crear un mejor *ambiente de bienvenida* en esta escuela para TODOS los padres?

_____

_____

_____

El comité de planificación repasará tus ideas y las ideas del foro para aumentar el involucramiento de todas las familias. El comité diseñará e implementará dos o tres actividades durante el siguiente año para fortalecer el programa de alianzas de la escuela, familias, y la comunidad.

¡Gracias por tus ideas!

CHAPTER 7
Series of Workshops

Chapter 6 described how workshops for parents may be organized as forums. Forums provide parents with opportunities to discuss their ideas with educators, other parents, and community members and to submit suggestions for improving school programs and activities.

This chapter shows how a *series of workshops* may be organized to help immigrant and other parents improve their understanding of the school, support their children's academic and social development, and build leadership skills to work with teachers and other parents on the school's program of family and community involvement.

Featured Activity International Parent Workshops

Patterson High School in Baltimore, Maryland, serves students and families who speak various languages at home, including Spanish, French, Swahili, Arabic, and Nepali. Many families are refugees from war-torn countries who arrived in the United States with the clothes they were wearing and little else. School leaders wanted to welcome the families, smooth the transition to their new country, and increase their involvement at school and in their children's education.

The partnership team developed *International Parent Workshops*—a series designed for new immigrant parents, although other parents were welcome to attend. Theme-based meetings were conducted once a month on Wednesday evenings from six to seven. At each meeting, two or three guest speakers shared their expertise with the families attending the workshop. One month, for example, a nutritionist spoke about healthy recipes that children and families would enjoy. Another month, a police officer discussed student behavior, preventing gang involvement, and what parents can do to protect their children. Parents shared their ideas, as well as their concerns and questions.

Teachers also served as guest speakers. They provided academic information and discussed ways that families can support and enhance classroom instruction at home in various subjects and at different grade levels. They highlighted club and after-school opportunities that students could join to build their interests and talents. They addressed parents' questions.

The school provided interpreters for parents who spoke languages other than English. It also provided transportation to the meetings and emergency food and clothing for families in need. The total cost to the school for the monthly meetings was $50 for one year. The Maryland Food Bank and the YMCA of Central Maryland assisted with monetary and in-kind donations.

Source: Adapted from Patterson High School, in D. J. Hutchins, *Promising Partnership Practices 2010* (Baltimore: National Network of Partnership Schools at Johns Hopkins University, 2010), page 60. Explore this and other ideas at www.partnershipschools.org in the section Success Stories.

You Try It!

Your school's planning committee may elect to conduct monthly *International Parent Workshops* to increase the involvement of diverse families in your school. This activity is appropriate for preschools and elementary, middle, and high schools. Here are a few things to consider.

Select Workshop Topics. The organizers of *International Parent Workshops* at Patterson selected topics for the monthly meetings that they believed would interest and benefit the parents at their school. Alternatively, you may survey parents for their suggestions of topics for workshops that they would attend. Some workshops address parents' concerns about parenting and about their children's learning or development. Other workshops introduce parents to important information about the school, district, or community. Your school's workshops should address topics that are tailored to parents and students at your school level.

Set a Consistent Schedule. If you organize a series of workshops, it is important that they are offered on a clear schedule (e.g., same day of the week, same time of the day or evening). One strength of *International Parent Workshops* was the consistency of the schedule (Wednesday evenings from 6 to 7 p.m.). If families know that there is a set time for workshops, more will set their own schedules to attend. Some schools repeat workshops for parents at different times (e.g., offer the same workshops in the morning and in the evening) to reach more and different parents.

Create Cohesion. A series of workshops should have a clear purpose—that is, the series should add up to new knowledge, positive attitudes, and productive involvement for the immigrant and other parents who attend. A well-planned workshop series will make parents feel welcome, provide useful information, enable them to share their ideas with other parents, and help them gain confidence about their involvement at school and in their children's learning and development. Although each session may stand on its own, there should be connections across sessions in the series. For example, at the end of one session, a workshop leader may challenge parents to use something they learned to guide their own student at home. At the start of the next workshop, parents may report whether and how they met that challenge.

Broaden Parents' Social Networks. About thirty-five parents regularly attended the *International Parent Workshops* at Patterson High School. Other parents attended one or a few workshops. School leaders and planners may increase attendance by using innovative and persistent advertising, by arranging carpools by neighborhood, and by encouraging parents to bring a friend to the next workshop. Some schools organize neighborhood representatives who speak the home language of parents in their areas. These volunteers alert a group of parents to workshops and other events at school, assuring them that volunteers will meet them there and serve as interpreters. These strategies increase attendance at workshops and help parents expand their social networks.

Choose a Convenient Location and Provide Transportation. Some parents may not have transportation to attend workshops at the school. Others, particularly immigrant parents, may not feel comfortable going to the school, going at night, or going alone. Your planning committee may find a community partner who will provide transportation for parents to attend a workshop. Some schools arrange car pools, which help parents meet other parents in their area. Some schools conduct some workshops in the community at a YMCA, community center, local church, district office, or other location that is convenient for many parents. Ultimately, for ease and for equity, it is important to help parents feel comfortable about going to workshops at their child's school.

A Different Design — Grow a Tree of Knowledge— Your School, Your Student, and YOU!

The monthly series of *International Parent Workshops* covered various topics that the planning committee believed were important for new immigrant, multicultural, and all other parents to know about and to discuss with teachers, community experts, and each other.

The alternative example, *Grow a Tree of Knowledge*, shows how to organize a short series of three workshops to help new immigrant parents and others who have been uninvolved in the past become acquainted with the policies and procedures of their child's school. This mini-course is designed to improve knowledge about the school, district, and community, thus increasing parents' readiness to participate actively as volunteers.

Workshop 1: Your School Tour

Purpose

Workshop 1 in the series, conducted at the start of the school year (or before school opens), is designed to familiarize parents with the school building, policies, programs, and technologies and with teachers' expectations. This workshop also aims to familiarize teachers with their students' families. The session addresses parents' questions about the school and provides parents who do not speak English with assistance in filling out school forms, such as emergency and contact information and applications for free and reduced-price meals.

Materials

- Pen or pencil for each participant
- *Leaf Pattern* (page 81)
- *School Tour* activity page (pages 82–83, English and Spanish)
- Map of the school
- School policies and procedures (i.e., a short, clear handout for parents in languages they can understand)
- Magnet or card with school contact information (address, phone number, website)

Planning

1. Prior to the workshop, ask school staff and faculty to serve as tour guides. Recruit enough guides to conduct small groups of five to ten parents who register for the workshop. Ensure that families who speak languages other than English will be grouped with a bilingual tour guide.

2. Prepare a tour guide's script for each stop of the tour. The script will ensure that the tour guides share the same information with all parents.

3. Plan for each guide to take a different route through the school so that the stops along the way are not too crowded. Decide on timing at each stop so that the tour proceeds on an orderly schedule.

4. Publicize *Your School Tour* with information in different languages for all incoming families to your school. Use the local multicultural media in your area, flyers, bilingual volunteers to call groups of parents, and other strategies discussed in Chapter 2.

5. Prepare or identify a short summary of major school policies and procedures, with translations as needed in parents' home languages.

6. Obtain magnets or cards with school contact information (e.g., main phone number, website).

7. Complete all planning for refreshments, materials for the workshop, and translation equipment, as needed.

Activity

1. At the workshop, give each parent a welcome packet with the materials listed above, including the summary of school policies and procedures, and the magnet or card with school contact information.

2. Provide a meal or light refreshments at the start of the time period. Invite the principal and the chair of the planning committee to welcome parents and explain the purpose of Workshop 1 in the series.

3. Conduct the icebreaker (*Tree of Knowledge*, pages 80–81). Summarize important ideas that the parents wrote on their leaves about how all parents may support their children as students at any grade level. Note that future workshops in the series will add more leaves to the growing tree.

4. Divide parents into groups of five to ten. Assign each group of parents to a tour guide. If several families speak a language other than English, provide a guide who speaks their language. The tour guides will take their groups of parents on the tour of the school, following the different, preplanned routes to avoid crowding.

5. At each location, the guide will discuss related policies, procedures, or other useful information. Parents will have five minutes to fill in their observations and reactions on their *School Tour* activity page. For example, when visiting the main office, the tour guide may introduce the school secretary, discuss attendance policies, show where volunteers and visitors sign in, give the school's phone number, and so on.

6. At the end of the tour, all groups will come together in the cafeteria or gym to discuss their reactions and their questions.

7. School staff and interpreters will assist all parents who need guidance, interpreters, or translations to complete required school forms (e.g., emergency cards, applications for free or reduced-price meals).

Workshop 2: Your District and Community Fair

Purpose

Workshop 2 in the series aims to acquaint parents with district and community resources that will help them support their children's learning.

Materials

- ◆ Summary of district and community resources and websites (short, clear handout for parents in languages they can understand)
- ◆ Presenters will bring information on their programs and services to distribute to parents.
- ◆ Leaves for each participant that will be added to the *Tree of Knowledge*

Planning

Prior to this workshop, invite key district office leaders and community organizations to provide information on their programs and services.

- ◆ For example, invite representatives from the YMCA, faith-based organizations, hospitals or clinics, public library, colleges, city council, and others to set up tables in the school cafeteria with clear and useful information for parents of students in your school.

- ◆ Invite members of the district's central office to set up displays and handouts on the district's parent involvement policy, advisory groups, and special academic, after-school, and summer programs for students.

Activity

1. Provide a meal or light refreshments.

2. Invite the principal and the chair of the planning committee to welcome parents and explain the purpose of Workshop 2 in the series.

3. Begin Workshop 2 by reviewing a few facts or results from Workshop 1. Check for remaining questions.

4. Explain that Workshop 2 is organized as a community fair. Participants will visit the various stations set up in the cafeteria or gym. Encourage parents to collect information and ask questions as they move from booth to booth.

5. After forty-five minutes, bring the attendees back together.

   ◆ Discuss how district and community resources can assist the families and help them support their children developmentally and academically.
   ◆ Discuss other programs and services not represented and where to find information about them.

6. At the end of the workshop, give each parent a leaf of a different color from Workshop 1. Ask them to write their ideas for the following statement:

   The most important thing I learned at the District and Community Fair Workshop was _____.

   Share some responses, and place the leaves on the growing *Tree of Knowledge*.

Workshop 3: Your Role in Your Child's Education

Purpose

Workshop 3 in the series will help parents crystallize ideas on ways to support their own children as students and become more actively involved at school and at home as a partner in education.

Materials

   ◆ Writing instrument for each parent
   ◆ Handouts of *Epstein's Six Types of Involvement* (short, clear handout for parents in languages they can understand) (pages 84–85, English and Spanish)
   ◆ Leaves for each participant that will be added to the *Tree of Knowledge*
   ◆ *Volunteer Survey* cards (page 86, English and Spanish)

Planning

1. Prior to Workshop 3, invite two or three teachers and two or three parent volunteers to speak at the workshop about different ways that parents may volunteer *at the school* and *for the school* at other locations (e.g., at home, in the community, at their workplace).

2. Because this is the last session of the mini-course, consider having a celebratory potluck dinner for which parents may bring food from their home countries or a favorite dish to share with others. This will take some planning by the planning committee with the parents who have attended the series of workshops.

Or continue the pattern from prior workshops of providing a meal or light refreshments at the start of the gathering.

Activity

1. Invite the principal and the chair of the planning committee to welcome parents and explain the purpose of Workshop 3 in the series.

2. Begin Workshop 3 with a review of the last session. Ask parents if they had an opportunity to use any of the district or community resources that they learned about at the *District and Community Fair* and if they have remaining questions.

3. Distribute the handout on *Epstein's Six Types of Involvement*.

4. Have the invited classroom teachers and administrators share examples of the six types of involvement activities that they conduct to help parents become involved in different ways.

5. Also ask parents for examples of how they activate the six types of involvement at home and in the community to support their children as students.

6. Invite parents to become volunteers to support teachers, administrators, and students at the school or in other locations by completing the *Volunteer Survey* card with information on their skills, talents, languages, availability, and preferred locations.

7. End Workshop 3 by asking parents to write their ideas to answer the following question on a leaf of a different color from those used in Workshops 1 and 2:

   *What is one **specific action** that YOU will take to support your child's educational success?*
   Share some responses, and place the leaves on the growing *Tree of Knowledge*.

8. Ask attendees to evaluate the Workshop Series on an exit evaluation (pages 140–141).

9. Send the *Volunteer Survey* card to parents who were not able to attend the workshop (e.g., send home with students, place in school newsletter as a tear-off, put on the website, or disseminate in another way). Include a friendly explanation to invite parents to become volunteers at the school or to assist the school as "at home" volunteers.

Icebreaker: Tree of Knowledge

Purpose

This activity gives participants an opportunity to share ideas about education and support for students.

Materials

- ◆ Pen or pencil for each participant
- ◆ Large poster of a tree with branches
- ◆ Tape
- ◆ *Leaf Pattern* (page 81)

Planning

Prior to the activity, draw a large tree with branches but no leaves on brown butcher paper. Cut it out and paste it on white paper with a title at the top, such as *Tree of Knowledge* or *We Grow Our Support for Education*. Make enough leaves on colored paper for each participant to have one for each workshop in the series.

Activity

1. At the start of Workshop 1, give each participant one leaf. Distribute them when the parents sign in or place leaves on each table.

2. After welcoming parents to the workshop, ask them to write their answer on the leaf to the following question: *What is one important way that YOU support your child **as a student?***

3. After a minute or two, ask a few parents to read their answers aloud for the group to hear different ways that parents support their children as students.

4. Ask the parents to tape their leaves to the *Tree of Knowledge*.

5. Attendees will add more ideas in the other workshops in the series, using different colored leaves each time. At the end of each workshop, ask:
   What is one important thing you learned from this session?
   How can you use this information to support your child as a student?
   This will create a colorful tree by the end of the short workshop series.

Source: Adapted from Grove Elementary School in Wisconsin Rapids, WI, in D. J. Hutchins et al., *Promising Partnership Practices 2010* (Baltimore: National Network of Partnership Schools at Johns Hopkins University, 2010), page 87.

Leaf Pattern

School Tour

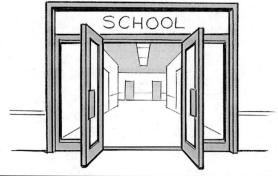

As you tour your child's school, write down something important or noteworthy about each location. Write questions that you have at each stop.

Location	What is important about this place?	What question do you have about this place?
Main Office		
Principal's Office		
Cafeteria		
Gym		
Playground		
Computer Lab		
Classroom		

Paseo por la Escuela

Direcciones: Mientras pasea por la escuela de su hijo(a), anote algo importante o interesante acerca de cada lugar. Apunte preguntas que tiene en cada parada.

Lugar	¿Qué es importante sobre este lugar?	¿Qué pregunta tiene sobre este lugar?
Oficina Central		
Oficina del Director(a)		
Cafetería		
Gimnasio		
Área de Recreo		
Salón de Computadoras		
Salón de Clase		

The Keys to Successful School, Family, and Community Partnerships:
Epstein's Six Types of Involvement

 **PARENTING:** Assist families in understanding child and adolescent development and in setting home conditions that support children as students at each grade level. Assist schools in understanding families.

 **COMMUNICATING:** Communicate with families about school programs and student progress through effective school-to-home and home-to-school communications.

 **VOLUNTEERING:** Improve recruitment, training, and schedules to involve families as volunteers and audiences at the school and in other locations to support students and school programs.

 **LEARNING AT HOME:** Involve families with their children in learning at home, including homework, other curriculum-related activities, and individual course and program decisions.

 **DECISION MAKING:** Include families as participants in school decisions, governance, and advocacy through PTA/PTO, school councils, committees, action teams, and other parent organizations.

 **COLLABORATING WITH THE COMMUNITY:** Coordinate community resources and services for students, families, and the school with businesses, agencies, and other groups, and provide services to the community.

Source: Epstein, J. L. et al. (2009). *School, Family, and Community Partnerships*, Third Edition and CD. Thousand Oaks, CA: Corwin Press.

Claves Para Las Alianzas Exitosas Entre Escuela, Familia, Y Comunidad:

Los seis tipos de involucramiento de Epstein

CRIANZA: Ayudar a las familias a comprender el desarrollo de los niños y adolescentes y a establecer un ambiente en casa que facilite el aprendizaje de sus hijos. Ayudar a las escuelas a entender a las familias.

COMUNICACIÓN: Comunicar a las familias sobre programas de la escuela y el progreso del estudiante a través de comunicaciones efectivas de la escuela a la casa y de la casa a la escuela.

VOLUNTARIADO: Mejorar el reclutamiento, entrenamiento y las oportunidades de voluntariado para involucrar a las familias como voluntarios y audiencia en la escuela y en otros sitios para apoyar a los estudiantes y programas de la escuela.

APRENDIZAJE EN CASA: Involucrar a las familias con sus hijos en el aprendizaje en la casa, incluyendo tareas, otras actividades curriculares, cursos, y decisiones de programa.

TOMA DE DECISIONES: Incluir a los padres como participantes en las decisiones escolares, el gobierno y la grupos de promoción a través de la PTA / PTO, los consejos de escuela, los comités, los equipos de acción y otras organizaciones de padres de familia.

COLABORACIÓN CON LA COMUNIDAD: Coordinar recursos y servicios de la comunidad para los estudiantes, las familias y la escuela con negocios, agencias y otros grupos. Proveer servicios a la comunidad.

Source: Epstein, J. L. et al. (2009). *School, Family, and Community Partnerships*, Third Edition and CD. Thousand Oaks, CA: Corwin Press. Spanish translation on CD.

Volunteer Survey

Note to Planning Committee: Customize this short survey to fit the needs of your school and families. A Spanish translation is below. Translate into the languages of your students' families.

VOLUNTEER SURVEY

Name of parent or family member: _____

Best phone number: _____ Best time to call: _____

E-mail address (if available): _____

I would like to help teachers ❏ in class ❏ on a trip ❏ contacting other parents

❏ I can translate notices from English to _____.

❏ I can serve as an interpreter for parents at school meetings or events in (language) _____.

❏ I would like to help the principal and staff in other locations (e.g., library, cafeteria, hallways).

❏ I would like to work one-on-one with a student on reading, math, spelling, mentoring, or _____
_____.

❏ I can share a talent or skill to enrich a lesson or club on occasion (please list): _____
_____.

Here are some times that I could assist at school (check ✓ all that apply):

Mon: AM_____ Tues: AM_____ Wed: AM_____ Thurs: AM_____ Fri: AM_____ On occasion_____

PM_____   PM_____   PM_____   PM_____   PM_____ Call to schedule_____

I am interested in volunteering at home (describe availability): _____

A member of the school's Planning Committee will call you about your schedule.

THANK YOU VERY MUCH!

ENCUESTA PARA VOLUNTARIOS

Nombre del padre o miembro de familia: _____

El mejor número de teléfono: _____ La mejor hora para llamarle: _____

Correo Electrónico (si tiene uno): _____

Me gustaría ayudar   ❏ En clase   ❏ En una excursión   ❏ Contactando a otros padres
a los maestros   ❏ Puedo traducir noticias al inglés del_____.

❏ Puedo servir como intérprete para padres en reuniones o eventos en (lenguaje) _____.

❏ Me gustaría ayudar al director(a) y al personal en otros lugares (e. g., biblioteca, cafetería, pasillos).

❏ Me gustaría trabajar con estudiantes individualmente en lectura, matemáticas, ortografía, ser
mentor, o_____.

❏ Puedo compartir un talento o habilidad para enriquecer una lección o club de vez en cuando
(favor de anotar talentos): _____.

Puedo asistir a la escuela durante estas horas (marque con un ✓ todas las posibilidades que aplican):

Lun: AM_____ Mar: AM_____ Mier: AM_____ Jue: AM_____ Vier: AM_____ De vez en Cuando _____

PM_____   PM_____   PM_____   PM_____   PM_____ Llamar para programar_____

Estoy interesado(a) en ser voluntario desde mi hogar (disponibilidad): _____

Un miembro del comité de planificación le llamará para coordinar.

MUCHAS GRACIAS!

CHAPTER 8
Promote Learning at Home

Parent involvement at school is *visible* to educators. Parent leaders, volunteers, workshop participants, and conference attendees are there—in school—easy to see. Parent involvement at home is sometimes *invisible* to educators and, therefore, overlooked. Yet parental involvement at home is very important for engaging all—not some—families and for increasing student success in school.

As schools develop their programs of family and community involvement, they must help immigrant parents—and all others—build their capacities to support their children's learning and development at home. One way to do this is to share information and ideas with parents about how to guide and support their children at home at all grade levels.

The following activity shows how one school introduced the school's writing curriculum to families at a parent workshop. One goal was to help parents understand how teachers teach writing to students in school. Another goal was to increase parents' confidence about discussing writing homework with their child at home. The activity shows how a workshop for parents may increase their involvement with students at home on curriculum-linked learning.

Featured Activity Opening Windows to Writing

Students became teachers—for a night—at Ranch View Elementary School in Naperville, Illinois. Their parents became students—for a night—getting acquainted with how the youngsters learn to write. Through a PowerPoint presentation starring its students and teachers, the school conducted *Opening Windows to Writing*, a session on the school's writing process.

This activity was part of a Back-to-School Curriculum Night—an event that normally draws up to 90 percent of the school's parents. The partnership committee decided to capitalize on the high attendance by featuring the school's writing curriculum and its high standards and goals for students' writing. That decision proved a good one. More than 400 parents and 50 faculty and staff members participated.

Teacher leaders—one for grades K–2 and one for grades 3–5—designed and delivered the PowerPoint presentation and accompanying handouts. The teachers videotaped students from each grade so parents heard the students, in their own voices, describing *six traits of good writing* and how they use them to learn to write better. The traits, used in many schools as part of the writing process, are *good ideas* (clear focus, purpose), *organization* (beginning, middle, end), *voice* (communicating with an audience), *word choice* (strong nouns, verbs, descriptors), *fluency* (flow of sentences), and *writing conventions* (grammar, spelling, punctuation). Students learn to examine their writing for these traits and strengthen their work where needed.

With these presentations, parents gained an understanding of how teachers taught writing in their classes and how the students applied the skills. They also learned the school's vocabulary, which they could use at home to ask their children about their writing homework.

One parent discovered that she already was on the right track with her primary grade student: "It made me realize I was doing the right thing by encouraging story writing, even at this age." High attendance at the event had an added bonus as the school's partnership team recruited several new members to plan and conduct other productive involvement activities to help increase student learning.

Source: Adapted from Ranch View Elementary School, in K. Salinas et al., *Promising Partnership Practices 2005* (Baltimore: National Network of Partnership Schools at Johns Hopkins University, 2005), page 16. Explore this and other ideas at www.partnershipschools.org in the section Success Stories.

You Try It!

Your school's planning committee may elect to conduct a workshop on a curricular topic that increases parents' understanding of how teachers work with students on specific school subjects and how parents can talk with and assist their children at home. If you implement a workshop like *Opening Windows to Writing*, here are a few things to consider.

Combine Events. Ranch View Elementary School capitalized on its established, well-attended Back-to-School Night to feature new information on the school's method of teaching writing across the grades. Consider combining a workshop on a subject in the curriculum with another event that, traditionally, brings large numbers of families to the school building. In addition to Back-to-School (or Open House) Night, this may be a major PTA/PTO meeting, a popular band concert, a sports activity, or a student assembly.

Remember Translators and Interpreters. If your school serves students and families who speak languages other than English at home, it is essential to have workshop materials translated prior to the workshop and to have interpreters at the workshop. Some schools conduct the same workshop in two rooms—one in English and one in Spanish. Also see Chapter 6 and other chapters for organizing translators and interpreters.

Use Technology. Technology is an important resource in classrooms and for communicating with parents. Consider new ways to show parents how teachers use new technologies to engage students using PowerPoint, streaming videos, SMART Boards, and other techniques. Also provide information on the school's website that parents and students may access at home or in the school or public library that extend the topics discussed at the Workshop for Parents.

Use Students as Teachers. Ranch View Elementary School featured videos of students completing and explaining their writing assignments. When students demonstrate their knowledge, skills, and talents, whether through videos or in person, more families attend a workshop. When students are "teachers" and parents are "students," more parents gain examples that can be replicated at home to support their children's learning. As an extra bonus, students tend to internalize what they teach.

Demonstrate Simple Strategies. Parents may have learned school subjects (e.g., math, reading, writing, science) differently from the way the subjects are taught in classrooms today. Family members benefit from clear advice and strategies on how to interact with and encourage their child in learning specific subjects at home. A useful workshop for parents combines information from teachers, examples of students' work, and the voices of students discussing their work to clarify how parents can help at home. Also, if your school adopts a new curriculum or new teaching approach, it is important to give parents some information on the new program and roles they may play to support their children's learning.

Get the Information from the Workshop to Parents Who Could Not Attend. Several items from the workshop *Opening Windows to Writing* could be sent home to parents who were unable to attend. For example, teachers might print and distribute the PowerPoint from the workshop and post the videos of students' presentations on the school's website. As another example, Highlands Elementary School, also in Naperville, Illinois, conducted workshops for parents on the state's writing standards and achievement tests, and how students learn different writing styles—narrative, persuasive, and expository. At the workshop, teachers conducted separate sessions for parents of students in grades K–2 and 3–5, provided information, showed students' writing samples, and prepared videos of the workshop for parents who could not attend to view at home (Salinas & Jansorn, 2003, page 21).

A Different Design Positive Homework Policies and Practices

The *Opening Windows to Writing* workshop was conducted at school, taught parents about the school's writing curriculum, and aimed to increase parents' confidence about helping their children at home. The alternative example shows how to organize a workshop at school, provide basic information to parents on how to help their child with homework, and provide the same information to parents who could not attend the activity at the school building. In this way, we redefine workshop from a meeting at school to the content of that meeting. This makes it possible for many more parents to attend to the content of the workshop than were able to attend the meeting, itself (Epstein et al., 2009).

Purpose

Conduct a workshop for parents on the school's homework policies and on positive strategies for helping their children at home. Extend the workshop to meet the challenge of providing information to those who could not attend. Provide all parents, regardless of home language, with ideas on how to encourage their children to discuss things they learned in class and to complete their homework assignments. These conversations help children see that their parents are interested in their education and support their learning at home.

Materials

- *Common Homework Questions & Answers* (pages 93–94, English and Spanish) This handout provides parents with common questions and answers about homework. It also may help parents think of other questions they would like to ask the panel of teachers, parents, and students.
- Monthly *Homework Hints* for parents (pages 95–98, English and Spanish) *Homework Hints* are basic suggestions that help parents establish positive conditions for students to complete their homework and encourage parents to have positive conversations with students about their classwork and ideas. A printed list of all *Homework Hints* will be distributed at the workshop and mailed to parents who do not attend. Thereafter, one hint will be distributed each month to all parents to highlight the importance of positive parent-child conversations about homework.
- Pens and pencils for workshop attendees
- Optional: Magnets (from an office supply store). The *Homework Hints* may be laminated and made into magnets to be mailed monthly with an explanatory letter and supplementary ideas. Alternatively, homework hints may be sent as monthly flyers or laminated bookmarks to call parents' and students' attention to positive support for homework.

Planning

1. Prior to the workshop, ask two teachers, two parents, and two students to serve on a panel about homework. For example, teachers from different grade levels may provide information about their homework policies, types of assignments, and how parents can help without "doing" the work. Parents representing those with different cultural backgrounds and with students at different grade levels may share successful strategies for talking about school and homework with their children. Students may describe their favorite homework assignments and ways their parents help them fulfill their homework responsibilities.

2. Identify one or two teachers who will work with two or three small groups of students to prepare brief, three- to five-minute skits about homework. These presentations may show some best vs. worst ways to help students complete their homework, discuss their work, or value school and homework. In a middle school, students may contrast best ideas for how parents can help on homework in the younger grades vs. the middle grades.

3. Invite parents to register (RSVP) to attend the workshop. Provide information on the topics that the panel will discuss and on students' related presentations. Encourage parents to come prepared with their own questions about homework.

4. Optional: Secure donations from community partners to provide dinner or light refreshments for parents who attend.

5. Make copies of the *Common Homework Questions & Answers* page for all participants.

6. Prepare the *Homework Hints* pages. Distribute the first one to attendees and send home to parents who were unable to attend.

7. Prepare fun and educational activities for students to complete while their parents attend the workshop.

Activity

1. As parents sign in, distribute the *Common Homework Questions & Answers* page to each participant.

2. Begin the workshop with dinner or light refreshments.

3. Invite the principal and the chair of the planning committee to welcome parents and explain the purpose and format of the workshop, with student presentations, panel, and Q & A with the principal and panel members. A school counselor may join the group for the Q & A period.

4. Have students present their homework skits. After the presentations, the students should meet for a planned activity while their parents are attending the workshop.

5. Present the panel of teachers, parents, and students. Each panelist should speak for about five minutes on their prepared topics (about thirty minutes for the six panelists). Then, the parents will have time for their questions.

6. During the panel discussion, audience members may write additional questions about homework.

7. Invite the principal to summarize main points about keeping homework time organized, positive, interactive, and productive at home. This summary should include what the school will do to help parents understand the homework policy, receive homework hints, get answers to any questions throughout the school year, and help their children enjoy school and learning.

8. After the workshop, distribute *Homework Hints* magnets or bookmarks to the parents in attendance. Provide the same materials to families who were unable to attend the workshop, either by mailing them home or sending them home with their student. One plan is to distribute *Homework Hints* monthly. Another option

is to create an attractive page of *Homework Hints* and distribute all of them at the same time for parents to read and use as needed.

Homework Hints Magnets: The planning committee or teachers may turn each hint into a magnet to post on a refrigerator or bulletin board at home. Here are two examples.

Homework Hint #1	Homework Hint #2
Talk with your child about the importance of education, schoolwork, and homework. **Discuss how your child may "take the role of student" by doing homework assignments.**	**With your child:** • **Set a regular time for homework.** • **Reduce distractions (e.g., turn off the TV and video games) during homework time.** • **Check that the homework is completed.**

Follow-Up: Evaluate the *Homework Hints* project to see if more students complete their homework over time, if students report more interactions on homework when a monthly Homework Hint is sent home, and if parents report that they feel more comfortable about guiding their students' homework completion. Check periodically to see if parents have more questions or suggestions for additional *Homework Hints*.

Common Homework Questions & Answers

Here are a few common questions and answers about homework. As YOU listen to the panel, jot down GOOD IDEAS that you hear and YOUR QUESTIONS about homework. You will be able to ask your questions of the principal, teachers, parents, and students at the end of the panel discussion.

Common Questions	Answers
Why is homework important?	Well-designed homework helps students review skills learned in class, extend their understanding of information, apply skills creatively, demonstrate their skills and share ideas with a family partner, and meet other learning goals. Homework helps students build useful study skills, work independently, take responsibility for their own learning, and understand their role as student.
How much time should my child spend on homework each night?	There is no single answer to this question. Time on homework will vary, based on your child's age, skills, and the design and purpose of the assignments. Young children (Grades K–2) may do 10 to 20 minutes of homework per night, but may read for pleasure for a longer time. Older elementary students (Grades 3–5) may do from 30 to 60 minutes of homework, or complete assignments in the time they need. Homework in middle school will vary by subject, purpose, and for different projects.
As a parent, how should I help my child with homework?	Your help will vary based on your child's age, needs, interests, and the teacher's advice. You can help your child by setting a regular time to complete homework, creating a quiet place for work and study, and showing real interest in your child's work and ideas.

Notes and Questions:

Contact your child's teacher if you have other questions about homework.

Source: Adapted from www2.ed.gov/parents/academic/help/homework/index.html.

Preguntas Comunes y Respuestas sobre la Tarea Escolar

Aquí hay algunas preguntas comunes y respuestas acerca de la tarea. Mientras que USTED escuche al panel, apunte IDEAS BUENAS que haya oído y SUS PREGUNTAS acerca de la tarea. Tendrá la oportunidad de hacer sus preguntas al director, maestros(as), padres, y a los estudiantes al final de la plática del panel.

Preguntas Comunes	Respuestas
¿Por qué la tarea es importante?	La tarea que está bien diseñada ayuda a los estudiantes a repasar las habilidades que aprendieron en clase, extender su entendimiento de la información, aplicar habilidades creativamente, demostrar sus habilidades y compartir ideas con un miembro de familia, y alcanzar otras metas de aprendizaje. La tarea ayuda a los estudiantes a construir hábitos de estudio útiles, trabajar independiente, tomar responsabilidad por su aprendizaje, y entender su papel como estudiante.
¿Cuánto tiempo debe pasar mi hijo/a haciendo tarea cada noche?	No hay una sola respuesta para esta pregunta. El tiempo haciendo tarea varia, dependiendo de la edad de su estudiante, habilidades, y el diseño y propósito de la tarea. Niños pequeños (entre grados K–2) deberían hacer tarea por 10–20 minutos cada noche, pero pueden leer por placer más tiempo. Los estudiantes mayores de primaria (entre los grados 3–5) deberían hacer tareas por 30–60 minutos, o completar tareas en el tiempo necesario. La tarea de la escuela secundaria variará dependiendo de la materia, propósito, y tipo de proyectos.
¿Como padre, cómo debería ayudar a mi hija/o con su tarea?	Su ayuda variará dependiendo de la edad de su hijo, sus necesidades, intereses, y los consejos del maestro(a). Puede ayudar a su hijo dándole un horario regular para completar la tarea, creando un sitio silencioso para trabajar y estudiar, y mostrando interés real en el trabajo e ideas de su hijo.
Notas y Preguntas: **Comuníquese con el maestro(a) de su hijo si tiene otras preguntas acerca de la tarea.**	

Fuente: Adaptado de www2.ed.gov/parents/academic/help/homework/index.html.

Homework Hints

Dear Parent or Guardian:

Here is a list of *Homework Hints* that may help you communicate with your student about homework in positive ways. Although these general suggestions apply to all grade levels, homework assignments and teachers' expectations will vary from grade to grade, subject to subject, and teacher to teacher.

If you have questions about your child's homework, contact the teacher for a conference or conversation.

Sincerely,
The Planning Committee
Workshop: *Positive Homework Policies and Practices*

How do I help my child complete the assignment?

You can help by letting your child know that homework is important, learning is important, and school is important. Tell your child that his/her "job" right now is to be a student and that includes completing homework. This gives your child the message that you, as a parent, value homework. With a clear and positive message, your child will value school, learning, and homework, too.

What is the best way to help with homework?

In addition to talking with your child about the importance of school and homework, the best way to help is to ask your child to show you how to do a particular math example, or read to you something he/she wrote, or discuss something interesting learned in a particular subject. When your child acts as a teacher and you listen as an interested partner, your child will be proud of his/her work and will see that you care about his/her ideas.

What if my child has a question about homework?

Some questions can be answered by jogging your child's memory. Review: What was the assignment? What were you learning in class? What did the teacher say to do for homework? Some questions can be answered by checking the directions in a book. If the assignment is on page 10, check the directions on page 9 for guidance and a related example.

Some questions can be addressed if your child calls a friend.

If you cannot answer your child's question, write a note to the teacher. Ask the teacher to help your child understand the assignment and give your child an extra day to complete the work, or to call you so that you will have an idea about how to help in the future.

What if I think there is too much or too little homework?

Teachers should explain their policies on homework at the start of the school year. If you missed that information, ask for a parent-teacher (or parent-teacher-student) conference to discuss the homework policy and the teacher's expectations.

How do I correct my child if he/she made homework errors?

Be careful, patient, and positive about pointing out errors. If something is incorrect, ask your child to double-check directions or examples in the book, or explain to you how he/she got an answer. By working step by step through a math problem or by reading a sentence aloud, many students will find their own errors. If you know how to guide your child in positive ways through the steps in a particular subject, of course, you should do so. If your child resists your assistance, let it go until the teacher checks the work. Both you and your child should check the teacher's comments on homework to make sure that your child understands how to proceed in the future.

What if my child likes to do homework with the radio or TV on or while listening to an iPod?

It is generally believed that homework should be done in a quiet place and without distractions. Some homework may be done with others in the area (e.g., around the kitchen table, on the living room floor). Some homework requires a student to interview a parent or to talk about things together. Most homework aims to help your child practice or perfect a skill or activity that was taught in class. Help your child see that the work will be completed fastest and most accurately in a quiet place. When homework is done, there should be time for friends, noise, and fun. In the higher grades, some students who have the homework habit and know it is helping them do better in school may prefer doing their homework in the library or in another available quiet spot.

What if my child is frustrated by the homework?

Sometimes an assignment is too hard for a student's skill level. This is a good time to request a parent-teacher (or parent-teacher-student) conference. Talk with the teacher about the student's skills and abilities. It helps the student to hear the teacher's confidence that he/she can do the work. If the homework is too easy, some students get bored and frustrated. Again, a discussion with the teacher may result in some challenging extra-credit activities to increase the student's interest in completing assignments.

What is the best way to help my child develop good homework habits?

If you start in first grade to help your child see that homework is interesting and fun to do, and continue that message each year, your child will develop good homework habits, will look to you for support and encouragement, and is likely to do his/her best in school. At the start of each year, talk with your child about your home rules about homework, about his/her goals for the school year, and about how you will help him/her reach those goals. It helps, too, to recognize or praise a good job—a neat paper, a completed task, an interesting report. Children respond to honest praise, when it is deserved for a job well done.

Source: Adapted from *Helping Your Child with Homework*, U.S. Department of Education, 2005. See other ideas online at www2.ed.gov/parents/academic/help/homework/index.html.

Consejos para la Tarea Escolar

Estimado Padre o Tutor:

Aquí está una lista de *Consejos para la Tarea Escolar* que le ayudará a comunicarse positivamente con su estudiante acerca de la tarea. Aunque estas sugerencias generales aplican a todos los grados, las tareas y expectativas de los maestros(as) variarán de grado a grado, materia a materia, y de maestro(a) a maestro(a).

Si tiene preguntas sobre la tarea escolar de su hijo, comuníquese con el maestro(a) para tener una conferencia o platica.

Sinceramente,
Comité de Planificación
Taller: *Políticas y Prácticas de la Tarea Positiva*

¿Cómo ayudo a mi hijo a completar la tarea?

Puede ayudar a su hijo/a demostrándole que la tarea es importante, aprender es importante, y que la escuela es importante. Dígale a su hijo/a que su "trabajo" ahorita es ser un estudiante y que eso incluye completar las tareas. Así, le da a su hijo el mensaje de que usted, como padre, valora la tarea. Con un mensaje claro y positivo, su hijo valorará la escuela, el aprendizaje, y a la tarea también.

¿Cuál es la mejor manera de ayudar con la tarea?

Además de hablar con su hijo acerca de la importancia de la escuela y de la tarea, la mejor manera de ayudar a su hijo es pidiendo que le muestre cómo hacer un ejercicio de matemática, que le lea algo que él/ella escribió, o que hable de algo interesante que aprendió en una materia. Cuando su hijo actúa como maestro(a) y usted le da atención como un aliado interesado, su hijo se sentirá orgulloso de su trabajo y verá que a usted le interesan sus ideas.

¿Qué pasa si mi hijo tiene una pregunta acerca de la tarea?

Se puede contestar algunas preguntas estimulando la memoria de su hijo. Pregúntele: ¿Cuál fue la tarea? ¿Qué estabas aprendiendo en clase? ¿Qué les dijo el maestro(a) que hagan de tarea? Se puede contestar algunas preguntas revisando las instrucciones del libro. Si la tarea está en la página 10, revise las instrucciones en la página 9 como guía y busque un ejemplo relacionado.

Algunas preguntas podrían ser resueltas si su hijo llama por teléfono a un amigo.

Si no puede contestar la pregunta de su hijo, escríbale una nota al maestro(a). Pídale que ayude a su hijo a entender la tarea y que le dé un día extra para completarla, o que le llame para que usted tenga una idea de cómo ayudar en el futuro.

¿Qué pasa si pienso que hay mucha o poca tarea?

Los maestros(as) deben explicar sus políticas de tarea al comenzar el año escolar. Si perdió la información, pida una reunión de padre y maestro (o padre-maestro-estudiante) para hablar de la políticas de tarea y para entender las expectativas del maestro.

¿Cómo corrijo a mi hijo si él/ella cometió errores en su tarea?

Ten cuidado, paciencia, y se positivo al señalar errores. Si algo está incorrecto, pídale a su hijo que repase instrucciones o ejemplos del libro, o que le explique cómo llego a la respuesta. Trabajando un problema de matemáticas paso a paso o leyendo una oración en voz alta muchos estudiantes encuentran sus propios errores. Si sabe cómo guiar a su hijo de manera positiva por los pasos en una materia, claro que lo debe hacer. Si su hijo resiste su ayuda, déjalo hasta que el maestro revise el trabajo. Su hijo y usted deben repasar los comentarios del maestro en la tarea para asegurar que su hijo entiende cómo avanzar en el futuro.

¿Qué pasa si a mi hijo le gusta hacer su tarea con la radio o televisión prendida o mientras escucha a un iPod?

Generalmente se cree que la tarea se debe hacer en un sitio silencioso y sin distracciones. Algunas tareas se pueden hacer con otras personas alrededor (e. g., en la mesa de la cocina, en el piso de la sala). Algunas tareas requieren que el estudiante entreviste a un padre o que hablen acerca de algunos temas. La mayoría de las tareas tienen la meta de ayudar a su hijo a practicar o a perfeccionar una habilidad o actividad que le fue enseñada en clase. Ayude a su hijo a ver que la mayoría de las tareas puede ser completada más rápido y con más precisión en un lugar silencioso. Luego de completar la tarea, debe haber tiempo para amistades, ruido, y diversión.

En los grados mayores, los estudiantes que tienen el hábito de hacer tareas y saben que las tareas ayudan a ser mejor en la escuela, podrían preferir hacer su tarea en la biblioteca o en otro lugar silencioso disponible.

¿Qué pasa si mi hijo esta frustrado por la tarea?

A veces la tarea es muy difícil para la habilidad y el nivel de un estudiante. Si esto sucede con frecuencia, pida una reunión de padre y maestro (o padre-maestro-estudiante). Hable con el maestro sobres las habilidades y capacidades de su estudiante. Al estudiante le ayuda escuchar la confianza del maestro que él/ella sí puede hacer el trabajo.

Si la tarea es muy fácil, algunos estudiantes se aburren o frustran. El hablar con el maestro podría resultar en que el estudiante recibirá actividades más desafiantes para aumentar el interés del estudiante en completar las tareas.

¿Cuál es la mejor manera de ayudar a mi hijo a desarrollar hábitos buenos para hacer la tarea?
Si empieza en primer grado a ayudar a su hijo a ver que la tarea es interesante y divertida, y continúa con ese mensaje cada año, su hijo desarrollará buenos hábitos para hacer la tarea, buscará su aliento y apoyo, y probablemente hará un mejor trabajo en la escuela. Al inicio de cada año escolar, converse con su hijo sobre las reglas de la casa sobre las tareas, las metas para el año escolar, y cómo usted le ayudará a alcanzar esas metas. También ayuda, reconocer o elogiar el trabajo bien hecho —un trabajo limpio, una tarea completada, un reporte interesante. Los niños responden a elogios honestos cuando son merecidos por un trabajo bien hecho.

Fuente: Adaptado de *Ayudando a Su Hijo Con la Tarea Escolar*, U.S. Department of Education,2005. Para más ideas visite www2.ed.gov/parents/academic/help/homework/index.html

PART FOUR

Curriculum Connections

Curriculum Connections begin in the classroom and reach out to engage families and students at home or in the community to enrich or extend students' learning.

What people are saying:

When I was a little girl in Venezuela, I had very long hair. I begged my mother to cut it for me and she did. What I did not know was that she had saved my hair clippings and put them into a bag, which she kept under her bed. After I married and . . . had my first daughter, my mother planned a trip to visit my new baby. She looked through some old things and found my braided hair. She decided to make a doll for me with the real hair. My daughter has chosen this doll as her family artifact.

Carolina Mendoza, Fifth-Grade Parent
L'Etoile du Nord French Immersion School, Saint Paul, Minnesota

---

Chapter 9: Family Involvement and Student Achievement

◆ *Amacca Museum* from Isaac Stevens Middle School in Pasco, Washington, describes how two sixth-grade teachers planned a culminating activity to get parents and other family members involved in a unit about Egypt.

◆ *Math in Our World* is an alternative design that gives all students and their parents an opportunity to think about the connections of school math skills and the use of math in everyday life.

Chapter 10: Engaging Families to Increase Student Learning

♦ *Understanding Culture and Identity Through Family Artifacts* from L'Etoile du Nord French Immersion School in Saint Paul, Minnesota, features an activity illustrating how this elementary school connected schoolwork with learning at home by having students study their heritage.

♦ *My Family Through the Years* is an alternative design that engages students with a family member in a social studies lesson on popular culture. It includes an interactive homework assignment for which students interview a family partner to compare and contrast everyday life for up to four generations of their family at the same age as the student.

Chapter 11: Family Involvement with Students: Reading at Home

♦ *Hooked on Books* from Roger Wolcott Early Childhood Center in Windsor, Connecticut, caught on as a reading incentive program for beginning readers. It involved real fish, paper fish, a contest, some science lessons, and books, books, and more books.

♦ *Literacy Bags* is an alternative design that encourages students and parents to enjoy reading together at home. The sample activities for grades K–2, 3–5, and 6–8 show teachers how to help parents and students discuss important ideas about diverse cultures.

CHAPTER 9
Family Involvement and Student Achievement

When the curriculum comes alive, students experience authentic learning. Project-based instruction gives students many opportunities to delve deeply into a subject. Then, students are eager to show and share what they learned with parents, other family members, and the community.

The featured activity, *Amacca Museum*, demonstrates how one school organized an exciting and important culminating activity for a major social studies unit that allowed students to share their knowledge with many others. The activity may be adapted to celebrate student learning in literature, the arts, and other subjects.

Featured Activity Amacca Museum

Taking a cue from the Smithsonian, sixth graders from Isaac Stevens Middle School in Pasco, Washington, transformed their cafeteria into a virtual Egyptian tomb. It was explored by over 300 parents on *Amacca Museum Night*.

Two sixth-grade teachers put their heads together to improve their unit on Egypt. They decided to help their students turn new knowledge gained in six weeks of studying mummies and hieroglyphs into an event that expanded beyond the classroom to get parents and other family members involved in the history lesson.

The teachers began the unit by dubbing their students young archeologists and inviting them to dig deeper into specific aspects of ancient Egyptian civilization. Students spent the next five weeks in class and in the library researching topics pertaining to ancient Egypt: daily life, the Nile Valley, religion, government, mummification, language, and pyramids. In the final week, the sixth graders worked in school and at home to create the artifacts that would showcase the information they had studied.

On the night of the *Amacca Museum*, 100 students managed twenty-eight different exhibits around the school cafeteria. Students had made statues of Egyptian gods out of clay and papier-mâché. They recreated burial masks, amulets, and clothing. They built a life-sized sarcophagus out of cardboard boxes and papier-mâché that visitors could lie in. In addition to the artifacts, students also developed several Egyptian-themed activities to entertain museum-goers. For example, they set up tables where parents and siblings could practice writing in hieroglyphics or play the ancient board game of Senet. Other displays invited parents to solve pyramid math puzzles and watch a puppet show about Egyptian gods and goddesses. All around the room, posters instructed parents on the timeline of Egyptian pharaohs and the hierarchy of the social classes. Several 3D models replicated the most important pyramids.

Parents, students, and teachers were thoroughly impressed with the content of the exhibit. Everybody involved enjoyed the collaborative atmosphere as students taught their parents many things about ancient Egyptian culture.

Source: Adapted from Isaac Stevens Middle School, in D. J. Hutchins et al., *Promising Partnership Practices 2008* (Baltimore: National Network of Partnership Schools at Johns Hopkins University, 2008), page 29. Explore this and other ideas at www.partnershipschools.org in the section Success Stories.

You Try It!

Your planning committee may support teachers' efforts to organize a culminating activity for a social studies unit that, like *Amacca Museum*, will involve all families in their children's learning about the world. Here are a few things to consider.

Adapt the Celebration of Learning to Other Subjects. In the *Amacca Museum*, students displayed the results of their studies and research on Egypt. The culminating activity allowed students to process, summarize, and share their new knowledge about many aspects of ancient Egyptian society in active, hands-on displays, games, and constructions. Visitors engaged in this museum as students made old Egypt come alive.

Similar and related designs can be developed for students to summarize and share the results of their work and new knowledge in any subject. As students' complete their work and share what they learn, their knowledge is internalized and becomes more meaningful to them. For example, eighth graders in McLoughlin Middle School, also in Pasco, Washington, read *Anne Frank: The Diary of a Young Girl* in language arts. The students, mainly Latino, also learned the history and culture of Europe and World War II, and developed live performances, art work, and constructions to share with other students, families, and the community in their *Vision of Hope Museum* (Hutchins et al., 2010, page 36).

Involve Families. Families supported students as they developed their projects, artifacts, and displays for the *Amacca Museum*. Family members provided advice and project materials, assisting students as needed, and attended the night at the museum to learn about and enjoy the students' work. In planning your school's culminating activity, ensure that families are involved in useful ways at various stages of students' work, not only in attending the celebratory event. Teachers may assign interactive homework that students conduct to keep families aware of their work and progress; request families to provide materials for students' projects; and request parents to serve as volunteers to help students display their projects.

Extend the Displays. *Amacca Museum* was "open" to visitors one evening. You may extend the time for displaying students' work and projects. You may invite other classes or grade levels in your school; invite your feeder school to visit during the school day; invite parents who could not attend the evening event to come at a convenient time; and invite the community to share in the celebration of learning by visiting the display during the day.

Modify for Other Grade Levels. Culminating activities that celebrate students' learning with high-interest, hands-on projects are appropriate for the elementary, middle, or high school grades. Younger students need more support and step-by-step guidance to transfer their own learning to an active form to share with others, but teachers and parent and community volunteers can help. For example, in L'Etoile du Nord French Immersion School in Saint Paul, Minnesota, third graders studied, wrote biographies, created art, and dressed as artists from different eras and countries. They shared their work in skits and displays (see the *Van Gogh Café* in Hutchins et al., 2010, page 35).

A Different Design Math in Our World

Amacca Museum Night was the culminating activity for a major social studies unit of work. This alternative activity shows how to engage students with their parents in math at the end of a math unit (grades 3–6). *Math in Our World* enables families to draw from their funds of knowledge to talk with students about how they use math in their everyday life. (See pages 9–10 for a discussion of funds of knowledge.)

Purpose

Math in Our World gives students an opportunity to think about the connections between school math skills and the use of math in everyday life. Students identify how they apply math skills in everyday activities. Then, they interview a parent to learn about their real-world applications of math at home, on the job, and in the community. The question and discussion—How do you use math?—may be asked in any language spoken at home and is meaningful for all parents and other family members, regardless of their occupations, interests, and talents.

As a culminating activity for a math unit, the focus may be limited to a specific math skill (e.g., how students and family partners use fractions, or addition, or measurement, or decimals). As a math motivator, the activity may focus on any or all uses of math in the real world.

Materials

- ◆ *Math in Our World* (pages 106–109, English and Spanish)
- ◆ Poster board for each student, about 12 x 14
  Prepare the poster boards for each student, as follows:
  - Write the title: Math in Our World
  - Draw a line down the middle of the poster to create two columns.
  - Label the top of the first column: I Use Math
  - Label the top of the second column: My Family Uses Math
  - Student will complete the poster by illustrating one example on each side.
  - If this is an end-of-unit activity, label the columns to feature a specific math skill (e.g., I Use Fractions/My Family Uses Fractions).
- ◆ *Math Journal* for each student

Planning

1. Provide a *Math Journal* for each student to use in class for one week. This may be a few pages to insert in students' notebooks or a small booklet labeled *Math Journal*. Two columns on each page should be headed:

    When did you use math?   **Which math skills did you use?**

    Students will record their experiences and name the math skills they use during the week.

2. Create a sample poster to show students good poster design.

Activity

1. For one week in math class, give students five minutes at the start or end of class to record in their *Math Journal* when and how they used math in the past day in their everyday lives and which math skills they used. Share one or two entries.

2. (Optional Activity) At the end of the week, just for fun, give out certificates to students with the most entries, silliest, most creative, most helpful, or other categories for their math connections.

3. At the end of the week, assign the interactive homework activity for students to interview a family member about their use of math at home, on the job, or elsewhere.

4. Reproduce or adapt and distribute the *Math in Our World* sheet. Go over the activity sheet with students, step by step, so they will know what to do when they complete the checklist about their own use of math, when they interview a parent or other family partner, and when they design a poster.

    • Go over page 1, which students complete on their own. Ask if there are any questions.

    • Go over page 2 (top), which is used when students interview a family member. Ask if there are any questions.

    • Go over page 2 (bottom) and discuss the purpose of the Poster Project. **Explain:** Students will review their *Math Journals*, the chart on p. 1 of the activity, and the information from their family partner to create a poster that highlights how they and their family member use math in their daily lives.

    The poster may be in English or in the students' home language (with translation to English). Discuss creative ways that students can represent the uses of math—for example, they may use bright colors to highlight their math examples, draw or photograph the situation where math is used, or cut and paste pictures from newspapers, magazines, or computer files to illustrate their uses of math. Show the students your pre-made sample of how an attractive poster will look.

- Give students at least three days to interview a parent and to complete their poster.

- Display the posters in math class or in a school location to share with other classes. Invite parents to a Math Gallery Walk to see the posters of all students' and families' math experiences in the real world. Students may help explain their posters on the Math Gallery Walk.

Math in Our World

Interactive Homework Activity

Name of student_____

Date due_____

It is fun to learn math in school every day.
Then, I use math in the real world—my way.
At home, we use numbers in things that we do.
Take a look—see how my family uses math, too!

1. **Think about how YOU use math at home or in other activities away from school.**

   Complete this checklist to tell how YOU use numbers in the real world.
   Check all the things you do with math and tell which math skills you use.

Check ✓ if you do these things.	Which math skill do you use?
I weigh myself.	
I play a game that needs math.	
I check sport scores.	
I follow a recipe.	
I go shopping.	
I garden.	
I save money.	
I plan my day and get to school on time.	
I save money to buy something I want.	
I watch my favorite TV show.	
I share a pizza with family or friends.	

2. **Add 2 more ways you use math or numbers at home and in other activities you do.**

   (1)_____ Which math skill?_____

   (2)_____ Which math skill?_____

3. **Write a sentence to tell: *How do math skills learned in school help you in everyday life?***

   _____

   _____

Family Interview

Members of your family know about math because they use numbers, too. Interview a parent or other family member about how he or she uses math in everyday life.

1. Whom are you interviewing?_____.

2. Show your family partner the checklist on page 1 and explain how YOU use math that you learned in school in the real world.

3. Ask your family member: *What are two ways that YOU use math at home, on the job, or in other activities? Which math skill do you use in each activity?*

My family member uses math to do THIS: **Which math skill is used?**

(1)_____   _____

(2)_____   _____

Your Poster Project

1. Choose **two** math connections to highlight—**one** way that **you** use math and one way that **your family partner** uses math in everyday life.

2. On the poster board, show the two uses of math that you selected.
   a. Sketch your poster in pencil on a separate planning page.
   b. Fill the whole space in each column of your poster so that others can see and enjoy your ideas.
   c. Make each column of the poster clear and interesting to look at.
      ◆ You may use colored markers to highlight your math examples.
      ◆ You may draw a picture, take a photo, or use pictures from a magazine, newspaper, or computer file to show where or how the math skill is used.
         ◆ Examples:
            ◆ If your family partner uses fractions in a favorite recipe, you might show the example of the fractions used and show your family member cooking.
            ◆ If you collect coins from your family's native country, you might show the value of coins in the collection and draw one or more of the coins.
   d. Complete your poster. Discuss it with a family partner. Bring it to school with this activity page on the due date. We will share and display the posters to see how math connects to everyday life.

Home-to-School Communication

Dear Parent/Family Partner:
Please share your reactions to your student's work on this activity.

Write YES or NO for each statement.

_____ 1. My child understood the homework and was able to discuss it.

_____ 2. My child and I enjoyed the activity.

_____ 3. This assignment helped me know what my child is learning in math.

Other comments: _____

Signature: _____

Source: Greenfeld, M. D., Epstein, J. L., and Hutchins, D. J., *Teachers Involve Parents in Schoolwork (TIPS): Interactive Homework for the Middle Grades* (Baltimore: Center on School, Family, and Community Partnerships, Johns Hopkins University, 2011).

Matemáticas en Nuestro Mundo

Actividad de Tarea Escolar Interactiva

Nombre del estudiante_____

Fecha de entrega_____

Es divertido aprender matemáticas en la escuela cada día.
Luego, uso las matemáticas en el mundo real—a mi estilo.
En el hogar, usamos números en cosas que hacemos.
Fíjate—¡mira cómo mi familia usa matemáticas también!

1. Piensa cómo TÚ usas matemáticas en el hogar o en otras actividades fuera de la escuela.

Completa esta lista para decir cómo TÚ usas números en el mundo real. Marca todas las cosas que haces con matemáticas y define las habilidades matemáticas que usas.

Marca ✓ si haces estas cosas.	¿Cuáles habilidades matemáticas usas?
Me peso.	
Juego un juego que usa matemáticas.	
Reviso resultados deportivos.	
Sigo una receta.	
Voy de compras.	
Trabajo en el jardín.	
Ahorro dinero para comprarme algo que quiero.	
Planeo mi día y llego a la escuela a tiempo.	
I save money to buy something I want.	
Miro mi programa favorito en la televisión.	
Comparto pizza con mi familia o amigos.	

2. Agrega 2 maneras más donde usas matemáticas o números en el hogar y en otras actividades que haces.

(1)_____ ¿Cual habilidad matemática?_____

(2)_____ ¿Cual habilidad matemática?_____

3. Escribe una oración explicando: *¿Cómo las matemáticas que aprendiste en la escuela te ayudan en la vida diaria?*

_____

_____

Entrevista Familiar

Los miembros de tu familia conocen las matemáticas porque ellos usan números también. Entrevista a un padre u otro miembro de familia sobre cómo él o ella usa matemáticas en la vida diaria.

1. ¿A quién entrevistaste?_____.

2. Muéstrale a tu miembro de la familia la lista de la pagina 1 y explícale cómo TÚ usas la matemáticas que aprendiste en la escuela en el mundo real.

3. Pregúntale a tu miembro de familia: *¿Cuáles son 2 maneras que TÚ usas matemáticas en el hogar, trabajo u otras actividades? ¿Cuál habilidad matemática usas en cada actividad?*

Mi miembro de familia usa las matemáticas para hacer ESTO:	**¿Cuál habilidad matemáticas se usó?**
(1)_____	_____
(2)_____	_____

Tu Proyecto de Cartel

1. Elige **dos** conexiones matemáticas para resaltar—**una** manera que **tú usas** matemáticas y **una** manera que tu **miembro de la familia** usa matemáticas en la vida diaria.

2. En el cartel, muestra los dos usos de matemáticas que seleccionaste.
   a. Haz un bosquejo en lápiz de tu cartel en una página separada.
   b. Llena todo el espacio en cada columna de tu cartel para que otros puedan ver y disfrutar de tus ideas.
   c. Haz cada columna de tu cartel clara e interesante.
      ◆ Puedes usar marcadores para resaltar tus ejemplos de matemáticas.
      ◆ Puedes dibujar una ilustración, sacar una foto, o usar una ilustración de una revista, periódico, o archivo de computadora para mostrar dónde o cómo se usa la habilidad matemática.
         ◆ Por ejemplo:
            ◆ Si tu miembro de la familia usa fracciones en una receta favorita, puedes mostrar un ejemplo de fracciones y mostrar a tu miembro familiar cocinando.
            ◆ Si juntas monedas del país de origen de tu familia, puedes mostrar el valor de las monedas en la colección y dibujar una o dos monedas.
   d. Termina tu cartel. Conversa con un miembro de la familia sobre tu cartel. Trae el cartel y esta página a la escuela en la fecha de entrega. Nosotros compartiremos los carteles para ver cómo las matemáticas se conectan con la vida diaria.

Comunicacion Hogar-Escuela

Estimado Padre/Miembro de Familia:
Por favor comparte sus reacciones sobre el trabajo de su estudiante en esta actividad.

Escriba Sí o NO en cada declaración.

_____ 1. Mi hijo entendió la tarea y fue capaz de hablar sobre ella.

_____ 2. A mi hijo y a mí nos gustó mucho esta actividad.

_____ 3. Esta tarea me ayudó a saber lo que mi hijo está aprendiendo en matemáticas.

Otros comentarios:_____

Firma:_____

Fuente: Greenfeld, M. D., Epstein, J. L., and Hutchins, D. J., *Teachers Involve Parents in Schoolwork (TIPS): Interactive Homework for the Middle Grades* (Baltimore: Center on School, Family, and Community Partnerships, Johns Hopkins University, 2011).

CHAPTER 10
Engaging Families to Increase Student Learning

In-depth classroom projects can extend learning into the home and help students discover and enjoy family memories and histories. Good projects tap parents' funds of knowledge and increase the involvement of all parents in their children's education (see pages 9–10). In these projects, language spoken at home is not an issue. Parents' formal education is not an issue. Transportation is not an issue. If students have a few days to connect with a family partner to complete the assignment, time is not an issue.

The featured activity shows how one elementary school connected schoolwork with learning at home by guiding students to study their heritage in a creative way.

Featured Activity Understanding Culture and Identity Through Family Artifacts

Handmade dolls, bracelets fashioned from silver spoons, and a great-grandfather's watch became the stuff of fifth-graders' stories, and eventually books, thanks to a project on family artifacts at L'Etoile du Nord French Immersion School, located in Saint Paul, Minnesota. *Understanding Culture and Identity through Family Artifacts* was a multidisciplinary project that involved language and arts curricula and tapped many resources, including parents, teachers, and community members.

Fifth-graders worked with their families to identify one artifact that had significant meaning to them and to their heritage. After choosing an artifact, each student talked with a family partner about the item and gathered the stories that surrounded it. The children interviewed their parents and other family members and wrote daily in a writer's notebook to practice and to improve personal narratives and descriptive writing. Eventually, each student produced several writings that were placed inside a handmade Family Artifacts box.

The students painted their 5 x 6 inch wooden boxes and topped them with marbled paper that they made themselves. Each box contained a fold-out map of the country from which the artifact came, a handmade book telling the story of the artifact written as realistic fiction, a family tree, and a handmade pamphlet describing the artifact in both English and French.

The project culminated with a celebration at the Minnesota Center for Book Arts. Students presented their artifacts on Family Artifact Day in May. Their parents, who were involved as resources and translators, also joined the celebration. One teacher concluded, "The fifth-grade teachers discovered that the books not only represented a student's culture and traditions, but also the unique fabric of our school community."

Source: Adapted from L'Etoile du Nord French Immersion School, in D. J. Hutchins et al., *Promising Partnership Practices 2008* (Baltimore: National Network of Partnership Schools at Johns Hopkins University, 2008), page 60. Explore this and other ideas at www.partnershipschools.org in the section Success Stories.

You Try It!

Your school's planning committee may elect to conduct a project for students to find and celebrate a family artifact, gain knowledge and history from a parent or other family member, and focus their writing, art, geography, and other learning on the family object and the story behind it. In this way, parents become involved in discussing family history and heritage with their child at home. They also may come to school to celebrate the completion of students' projects. If you implement something like *Understanding Culture and Identity Through Family Artifacts*, here are a few things to consider.

Encourage Authentic Learning Opportunities. *Understanding Culture and Identity Through Family Artifacts* is an excellent example of a project that asks children to tap into their families' funds of knowledge to learn about their heritage and family stories in a meaningful way. Variations on this theme may focus on a family hero, a family journey, or a family story without attention to a specific artifact. The student interviews a parent, grandparent, other relative, or older sibling for the family story. In all cases, such projects personalize the assignments so that each student explores his or her own family's heritage.

Interdisciplinary Connections. One strength of *Understanding Culture and Identity Through Family Artifacts* is that it builds students' skills in several subjects—literacy, social studies, and art. In this or similar activities, students may increase their knowledge and abilities in reading, writing, art, mapmaking, geography, history, and specialty subjects such as cooking, fashion design, film, and many more. Well-designed, hands-on projects may enrich student learning, increase parent involvement, and improve school, family, and community connections.

Use Unique Supplies. In the original activity, students decorated wooden boxes for their projects to ensure that all parts—artifacts, maps, original books, and other papers—were presented to their families in an artistic container. If necessary, students may use shoe boxes or surplus boxes donated from community businesses.

Showcase Projects. The featured project culminated in a way that involved students, families, and the community at a scheduled public event. This enabled students to share what they learned with a large, receptive audience. As you plan your project, be sure to allow students to share their work in meaningful ways at school or in the community—for example, by inviting other classes, other schools, families, and/or community members to celebrate the results of students' projects.

A Different Design **My Family Through the Years**

Understanding Culture and Identity Through Family Artifacts provided students an opportunity to study a family artifact and write creatively about its history and meaning to the family. As an interdisciplinary activity it helped students to build skills in writing, social studies, and art.

The alternative example, *My Family Through the Years*, is a Curriculum Connection that engages students in grades 3 to 8 with a family member in a social studies lesson on popular culture. It includes an interactive homework assignment in which students interview a family partner to compare and contrast everyday life for up to four generations of family members at the same age as the student. The family members (i.e., student, parent, grandparent, and great-grandparent) may have lived, as a child, in different countries or locales.

Purpose

Students will interview a parent and other family members (if they are available) to discuss how life was the same or different from today when their relatives were the student's current age. They will use the information to think about popular culture at different times and to compare the past with their own experiences.

Materials

- ◆ Pictures of cars, clothes, telephones, hairstyles from different decades
- ◆ Samples of music from different eras
- ◆ *Homework Instruction Page* (pages 114–115, English and Spanish)
- ◆ *My Family Through the Years* activity page (pages 116–117, English and Spanish)
- ◆ Art supplies as needed (paper, markers, crayons)

Planning

1. Prepare photos or other pictures (e.g., obtain from the Internet or make copies from books or magazines) for a social studies lesson about popular culture from at least three different eras.

2. Acquire poster paper and other supplies for students to complete their projects at home.

3. Make copies of the *Homework Instruction Page* for each student. Adapt the instructions and the chart, *My Family Through the Years*, to match your curriculum and your students' skills and interests.

Classroom Activity

1. To introduce this project, use the pictures and artifacts collected from three different eras or three decades with distinctive fashion styles. For example, you may have pictures of poodle skirts (1950s), bell-bottoms (1960s), and jeggings (2010s). Put the pictures on display and ask students to describe the similarities and differences that they see.

    For more information, see Fashions by Decade at www.factmonster.com/ipka/ A0878570.html.

2. Teach a lesson about changes in popular culture across generations. Link to current events, inventions, new technologies, or other subjects.

3. Review with students the homework assignment to compare their own cultural favorites with their relatives' when the family members were the same age as the student.

Homework Assignment

1. This assignment is appropriate for students starting in grade 3. See example of how to adjust and advance the activity for students in grades 6–8 (pages 114–115).

2. Print the instructions for the student and a family partner.

3. Give students at least three days to have time to interview a parent and complete the assignment.

4. Have some or all students present their most interesting findings in class.

5. If there is interest, display the pictures that students draw on a school bulletin board to share with students in other grade levels. If the pictures are drawn with care, consider an exhibit of the drawings and narratives in the community (e.g., at the YMCA, senior citizen's program, or public library).

Homework Instruction Page
(Grade 3 and above)

1. Complete the activity *My Family through the Years*.

   ♦ Interview a parent or other adult in your family about what that person's life was like when he/she was your age.

   ♦ Ask your parent about his/her parents (your grandparents) and parents' parents (your great-grandparents). Go back only as far as your family partner remembers.

   ♦ Discuss how each generation lived life at your age.

2. Select ONE heading on the chart that interests you.

   For that heading, draw or paint a picture comparing your life today with the life of ONE of your relatives (parent, grandparent, or great-grandparent) when he or she was your age.

3. For the heading you selected and the picture you drew, write one or two paragraphs to tell what you learned about the similarities and differences between YOUR life today and the life of the relative featured in your picture.

4. **Students in grades 6–8, add the following:** For the heading you selected, write a paragraph or two predicting what you think life will be like for a child your age in the year 2050.

Pagina de Instrucción para la Tarea
(Grado 3 y arriba)

1. Completa la actividad Mi Familia a través de los Años.

   ◆ Entrevista a un padre u otro adulto de tu familia sobre la vida de esa persona cuando tenía tu edad.

   ◆ Pregúntale a tu padre sobre sus padres (tus abuelos) y padres de sus padres (tus bisabuelos). Averigua hasta donde tu miembro de la familia se recuerdo.

   ◆ Discute cómo cada generación vivió cuando tenía tu edad.

2. Selecciona UN título que te interesa de la tabla en la página siguiente.

   Para ese título, dibuja o pinta una ilustración comparando tu vida de hoy con la vida de UNO de tus parientes (padre, abuelo, o bisabuelo) cuando él o ella tenía tu edad.

3. Para el título que seleccionaste y la ilustración que dibujaste, escribe uno o dos párrafos sobre lo que aprendiste de las semejanzas y las diferencias entre TU vida de hoy y la vida de tu pariente en tu ilustración.

4. **Estudiantes en los grades 6–8, agrega lo siguiente:** Para el título que seleccionaste, escribe uno o dos párrafos describiendo cómo piensas que la vida de un niño de tu edad en el año 2050 será.

My Family Through the Years

Talk with one or more family partners about how life was different from today when various family members were your age.

Use the table to summarize information from the PAST. In the bottom row, YOU describe YOUR life and favorites at PRESENT.

Year and location when relative was YOUR age	What transportation was popular?	What music was popular?	What clothing styles were popular?	What hairstyles were common?	How did students communicate with others?
Parent Year: City, State, Country:					
Grandparent Year: City, State, Country:					
Great-Grandparent Year: City, State, Country:					
YOU! Year: City, State, Country:					

Mi Familia a través de los Años

Habla con uno o más aliados familiares sobre cómo la vida fue diferente cuando ellos tuvieron tu edad y la vida de hoy.

Usa la tabla para resumir la información del PASADO.
En la última área de abajo, describe TU vida y TUS favoritos del PRESENTE.

Pariente a TU Edad (Anota el año y el local.)	¿Qué tipo de transporte fue popular?	¿Qué música fue popular?	¿Cuáles estilos de ropa fueron populares?	¿Cuáles peinados fueron comunes?	¿Cómo se comunicaban los estudiantes…con los padres? con otros estudiantes?
Un Padre **Año:** **Ciudad, Estado, País:**					
Un Abuelo **Año:** **Ciudad, Estado, País:**					
Un Bisabuelo **Año:** **Ciudad, Estado, País:**					
TU! **Año:** **Ciudad, Estado, País:**					

CHAPTER 11 ──────────
Family Involvement with Students: Reading at Home

It is critical for educators to share information with parents about how important it is for students to read for pleasure at home. Reading—like shooting baskets and playing the piano—is a skill that gets better with practice. Many studies confirm that students who enjoy reading books, newspapers, or magazines every day are better readers in school.

Featured Activity Hooked on Books

Are you looking for a fresh way to encourage children's reading for pleasure? *Hooked on Books* caught on as a reading incentive program for beginning readers at the Roger Wolcott Early Childhood Center in Windsor, Connecticut. It involved real fish, paper fish, a contest, some science lessons, and books, books, books.

During the month of May, children in the preschool and kindergarten at the Wolcott Center were encouraged—even more than usual—to read books at school and at home. Each time students read a book or were read to, they wrote their names on a paper fish. At the end of each week, the fish were "caught" and the class that netted the most fish was declared the week's winner. The prize? An opportunity to take care of the center's pet fish—Hook 1 and Hook 2. These two betta fish share a tank in the Family Resource Center (FRC) when they are not visiting a winning classroom of readers.

The FRC leader, who organized and promoted the incentive program, asked the owners of a local pet store to supply the fish—four in all—two in each hallway during the contest. The owner agreed and even offered to replenish the supply, if needed. Teachers kept talking with their students about the reading program. The FRC leader visited each class to build interest and encouraged parents to read with their children. The baskets of "caught fish" were displayed in the school foyer to kindle more interest.

Parents helped by reading to their children at home and by volunteering to prepare and supply the paper fish to meet the children's needs. The pet store staff got caught up in the spirit of the program, too, and shared tips for taking care of the donated fish. The pet store now proudly displays a certificate of appreciation from the Wolcott Center for being a community partner for *Hooked on Books*.

One family at the school donated a children's book for each classroom about the care and feeding of fish. The FRC leader read it to each winning class when she delivered the fish each week. Every classroom had a chance to win during the month.

By reinforcing a love of reading, teachers and parents helped students stay involved and excited about reading for pleasure. Making it a game added to the fun. Teachers not only saw children's interest in reading growing, but also had an opportunity to teach those science lessons about caring for fish.

Source: Adapted from Roger Wolcott Early Childhood Center, in D. J. Hutchins et al., *Promising Partnership Practices 2007* (Baltimore: National Network of Partnership Schools at Johns Hopkins University, 2007), page 13. Explore this and other ideas at www.partnershipschools.org in the section Success Stories.

You Try It!

The Roger Wolcott Early Childhood Center plans and implements many family and community involvement activities that link to school goals for improving students' reading skills and attitudes in the early grades. This activity, *Hooked on Books*, can easily be adapted in elementary and middle schools. If your planning committee for involving all families elects to organize a *Hooked on Books* project to encourage students to read for pleasure, here are a few things to consider.

Capture the Interest and Involvement of Multicultural Families. The staff at the Wolcott Center worked with the leader of the Family Resource Center to develop a creative way to hook young children on reading or listening to a parent read many books. This was done in a nonthreatening way that was easy for family and community members to support. In schools with families from different cultures and countries, the school or public librarian can develop an age-appropriate list of books that feature characters from many nations. By knowing your families and students and by planning ahead, you can help all students read more and better books.

Make It Visual and Tangible. With the theme *Hooked on Books*, the school, parents, and community made it possible for students to see how many books students read or heard using the paper fish shapes to record their experiences. Everyone could see the "school of fish" growing. Everyone could contribute by reading more. Having beautiful live fish from the pet store added to the fun.

The annual books of *Promising Partnership Practices*, produced by the National Network of Partnership Schools, share many other good ideas for encouraging students to read for pleasure. For example, in one school students wrote their names and the titles of the books read on the segments of a Book Worm that stretched around their classroom. Creative educators will easily develop other themes.

Make It Competitive. Everyone enjoys a healthy competitive game that has many winners. In *Hooked on Books*, different classes could "win" the chance to have Hook 1 and Hook 2 in their classrooms for a week. Other schools have held reading contests that led to a silly conclusion (e.g., if students read 1,000 books in a set time period, the principal will kiss a pig, paint the school logo on his or her forehead for a day, or be taped to the wall). The goal is to increase students' reading for pleasure, engage families in motivating students to read, and have some fun! And all students win by increasing their reading skills and good reading habits.

Make it NON-Competitive. Not every good program to encourage reading is set up as a contest. For example, Meadow Glens Elementary School in Naperville, Illinois, called its reading initiative *Expand Your World*. Parents received a list of multicultural books by grade level compiled by a local children's bookshop. (Lists of books written in different languages or set in different countries and times in history could also be developed by the school or public librarian.) Parents and children selected one multicultural book, read it together, and then created a book-jacket highlighting something about the country, culture, and experiences in the story. There was no contest—a celebration to share the book jacket designs was more fun because every student's artwork was on display.

Make Families' Roles Meaningful. *Hooked on Books* encouraged families to read to their young children at home. Students listed the books they read and those they listened to. This approach would work at least through second grade, since parents and teachers continue to read many short picture books to elementary school students. Students' lists included stories they read or heard in any language, since many parents read books in their native language and books they enjoyed as a child. Reading together can easily become a habit at all grade levels as families build close bonds by sharing good stories in any language, taking turns reading aloud, and talking about the characters they meet along the way.

Collaborate with a Community Partner. Following the program's theme, the FRC leader asked the local pet store to be a part of this project. The store contributed beautiful, live betta fish and other services. Community partners (e.g., businesses, agencies, service organizations) are more likely to support school projects that are goal-linked (here, on reading), well planned, and with many opportunities for students and parents to participate (not just a few). Your school's planning committee should ask for goods or services that a business or community partner can easily contribute to support a school program, not necessarily funds. Like *Hooked on Books*, your project may show its appreciation with a certificate from the school, a thank-you in the school newsletter, or some other public notice that students, educators, parents, and others in the community will see.

A Different Design Literacy Bags

Studies show that children in middle-income neighborhoods have many more books at home than do children in low-income neighborhoods. When funds are low, families may not be able to buy children's books. Schools and community projects can increase students' access to books to read for pleasure at home. The activity *Hooked on Books* was a special project conducted over one month. By contrast, *Literacy Bags* is an ongoing or periodic activity that encourages students and parents to enjoy reading together and talk about the books they read.

Purpose

Literacy Bags guide students and parents (or other family partners) to read and talk about books and stories at home. One goal is to increase students' interest in reading for pleasure. Another is to help parents develop skills and strategies to discuss a story and to prompt students to share their ideas about characters and events. *Literacy Bags* may provide opportunities for students to increase their understanding of the wider world by reading multicultural books set in other countries and other times in history.

Materials

- ◆ Age-appropriate, high-quality books
- ◆ Map of the world or the book's setting (optional)
- ◆ Activity pages for parents to (a) explain the *Literacy Bags* project and (b) guide parent-child interactions about the book in each bag (pages 124–135, English and Spanish)

Planning

1. Discuss the *Literacy Bags* project with participating reading teachers. Participating teachers will decide how many books and bags should be developed for each grade level. They may decide to use duplicate *Literacy Bags* so all students read the same book with their families at the same time. For example, teachers may select eight or nine books with enough copies for all students and parents to read one each month over the school year. Or teachers may create many different *Literacy Bags* so that each student can select a different book of interest each month. Or teachers may develop a different schedule of assignments for reading for pleasure at home.

2. Select the books for each grade level and purchase the books and bags.

3. Identify a time period for teachers (and/or district reading curriculum leaders) to develop laminated content cards or replaceable printed pages to guide students and parents in reading and discussing the books at home. The completed activities may also require other materials (e.g., marked world maps highlighting the countries where stories take place).

    The guide in each *Literacy Bag* will ensure that parents and students have positive reading experiences and conversations. Parents will gain an understanding of their child as a student and reader as they develop grade-appropriate strategies in how to read with their child, how to listen to their child read, and how to ask probing questions that spark their child's interest and ideas about a book. These skills can be used in conversations about other books the child reads.

4. Identify each bag so that the students, parents, and teachers know which book is in each *Literacy Bag*. Teachers may develop a sign-out/sign-in process for their grade levels.

See pages 124–135 for examples of guides for three books in *Literacy Bags* for students in grades K–2, 3–5, and 6–8. The three examples encourage students to read about characters with diverse cultural backgrounds.

> *Koala Lou* takes place in Australia. It features themes about the love and care in a family and children's goals for success. Koala Lou's mother becomes so busy raising many children that she forgets to tell Koala Lou how much she loves her. Koala Lou decides to train for the Olympics in order to win an event and capture her mother's attention and love. Her wins and losses provide many topics to discuss. (For grades K–2)

> *Masai and I* introduces students to the Masai—a unique people in Kenya, Africa. This is a wonderful book for comparing cultures. Linda, an African American girl in urban America, wonders how her life would be different if she were a Masai. The illustrator shows her dreams side by side—with pictures of daily life in the two cultures. (For grades 3–5)

> *Sing Down the Moon* is historical fiction about Native Americans. Named "outstanding book of the year" by the *New York Times* when it was published, the book provides many themes for students to discuss with a family partner. The story contrasts the Navaho tribe's original freedom in Arizona with the hardships of The Long Walk, the forced relocation of the tribe in the mid-1860s. (For grades 6–8)

Teachers may use or adapt these examples and prepare similar guides to accompany the books they select for their students.

Resources for Teachers

Michigan State University Libraries and School of Education periodically update their lists of recommended children's books with multicultural settings and provide other helpful websites. Visit http://libguides.lib.msu.edu/multicultural. Another resource is the University of Missouri's list of excellent children's books at http://ethemes.missouri.edu/themes/1499.

Activity

1. Explain *Literacy Bags* to the students and parents, including the purpose, schedule for reading books for pleasure at home, homework activities, and how a parent may contact the reading teacher with any questions.

2. Ask students to select a book for the month.

3. Introduce the activity each month and discuss the students' job of sharing the book with a family partner and completing the home assignment at the end of each activity.

Reinforce the goal that each student and family partner (e.g., parent, grandparent, older sibling) should enjoy sharing the book, reading for pleasure, and talking about their ideas.

4. Give students enough time to complete the reading activity, discussion, and homework assignment with a family partner. In class, on the due date, review the books and encourage students to share their thoughts about the books they read. Collect the homework assignment, grade it, and return it within a reasonable time.

5. Evaluate the project periodically, with reactions and suggestions from students, parents, and teachers.

Literacy Bag (Grades K–2)

Koala Lou, *written by Mem Fox and illustrated by Pamela Lofts*

Materials in the Bag

- Simple map of the world with Australia clearly labeled
- Guide for the student and parent or family partner to use when reading and discussing this book

Parents

Suggestions for topics and questions to discuss with your child are in italics. Add your own ideas to enjoy the book with your child.

Before Reading

This story is set in Australia. Let's look at the map in your bag and find Australia.

Explain

This story is about a koala and her family. A koala is a marsupial—as is a kangaroo. A marsupial mother carries her babies in a pouch or pocket on her tummy. Marsupials take good care of their babies and help them grow up in Australia.

Discuss

What are some ways that I (mother, father, or grandparent) take care of you and other members of the family? How do I help you grow up? How do you help yourself?

Introduce the Story

In this story, Koala Lou likes sports. She decides to build her skills climbing "gum trees" to enter the Olympics—a big sports event held in the Australian bush (a rural area with shrubs and trees). What sports do you like? How would someone get ready for a big contest like the Olympics?

Read Koala Lou

Let's find out…

- ◆ *How did Koala Lou's mother take care of Koala Lou and her many brothers and sisters?*

- ◆ *How did Koala Lou try to gain her mother's approval?*

When you reach the part of the story where Koala Lou starts training, stop reading and do some exercises together. Touch your toes. Try some sit-ups. Run in place. Then continue reading.

What do you think Koala Lou is trying to do?

Do you think her Mom still loves her, even if she doesn't have much time to say so?

What do you think will happen at the Bush Olympics?

Let's see what happens in the story.

After Reading

Even though Koala Lou didn't win the race, what did she win?

What are some ways that our family shows that we love and take care of each other?

Homework Activity for Students
Ask your child to choose <u>ONE</u> of the following homework activities to complete and bring back to class.

1. *There are many unusual animals in Australia. Let's look over the pictures in the book.*

   Can you find a colorful parrot, kangaroo, platypus, and kookaburra bird? What other animals do you see?

   a) Draw a picture of your favorite Australian animal.

   b) Write one sentence under the picture about why you think this animal is interesting.

2. *This story is about Koala Lou and what she really likes to do. She likes to climb trees!*

   a) Draw a picture of something you really like to do.

   b) Write one sentence under the picture about why you like to do this activity.

Bolsa de Lectura (Grados K–2)

Koala Lou, escrito por Mem Fox e ilustrado por Pamela Lofts

Materiales en la Bolsa

- ◆ Una mapa sencillo del mundo con Australia claramente marcado
- ◆ Guía para el estudiante y el padre o miembro de la familia para usar cuando se esté leyendo y conversando sobre el libro

Padres

Sugerencias de temas y preguntas para conversar con su hijo están en letra cursiva. Agregue sus propias ideas para disfrutar el libro con su hijo.

Antes de Leer

Este cuento sucede en Australia. Miremos el mapa en tu bolsa para encontrar a Australia.

Explique

Este cuento se trata de un koala y su familia. Un koala es un marsupial—igual como es un canguro. Una madre marsupial carga a sus bebés en una bolsa o petacón en su barriga. Los marsupiales cuidan muy bien a sus bebés y les ayudan a crecer en Australia.

Conversa

¿Cuáles son algunas maneras que yo (madre, padre, o abuelo) te cuido a ti y a otros miembros de la familia? ¿Cómo es que te ayudo a crecer? ¿Cómo te ayudas a ti mismo a crecer?

Presentar el Cuento

En este cuento, a la Koala Lou le gustan los deportes. Ella decide desarrollar sus habilidades trepando Eucaliptos para entrar en las Olimpiadas—un gran evento de deportes en el campo de Australia (una área rural con arbustos y árboles).

¿Cuáles deportes te gustan? ¿Cómo una persona se prepararía para un gran concurso como las Olimpiadas?

Lee Koala Lou

Hay que encontrar…

- ◆ *¿Cómo la mamá de Koala Lou cuidó a Koala Lou y sus varios hermanos y hermanas?*

- ◆ *¿Cómo Koala Lou intentó obtener la aprobación de su mamá?*

Cuando llegas a la parte del cuento en donde Koala Lou empieza a entrenar, deja de leer y haz ejercicios juntos. Toca tus dedos del pie. Intenta algunos abdominales. Corre en el mismo lugar sin avanzar. Luego sigue leyendo.

¿Qué piensas Koala Lou está intentando hacer?

¿Piensas que su mamá todavía la quiere, aunque no tiene mucho tiempo para decírselo?

¿Qué piensas sucederá en las Olimpiadas de Campo?

Veremos lo que sucede en el cuento.

Después de Leer

Aunque Koala Lou no ganó la competencia, ¿qué es lo que sí ganó?

¿En qué formas nuestra familia demuestra que nos queremos y nos cuidamos unos a otros?

Actividad de Tarea para los Estudiantes
Haz solamente <u>UNO</u> de lo siguiente:

1. *Hay una variedad de animales inusuales en Australia. Hay que mirar las ilustraciones en el libro.*

   ¿Puedes encontrar un loro de colores, un canguro, un ornitorrinco, y una cucaburra? ¿Qué otros animales encuentras?

   a) Dibuja tu animal Australiano favorito.

   b) Debajo de la ilustración, escribe una oración explicando porque piensas que este animal es interesante.

2. *Este cuento se trata de Koala Lou y de lo que a ella le encanta hacer. ¡Le encanta trepar árboles!*

   a) Dibuja algo que a ti te encanta hacer.

   b) Debajo de la ilustración escribe una oración explicando porque te gusta hacer esta actividad.

Trae la ilustración y la oración a tu escuela.

Literacy Bag (Grades 3–5)

Masai and I, written by Virginia Kroll
and illustrated by Nancy Carpenter

Materials in the Bag

◆ Map of the world with Africa, Kenya, and the Masai area in southern Kenya clearly labeled

◆ Guide for the student and parent or family partner to use when reading and discussing this book

Parents

Suggestions for topics and questions to discuss with your child are in italics. Add your own ideas to enjoy the book with your child.

Before Reading

This story is about one part of Africa and one group of people in that area.

Let's look at the continent of Africa on the map. Kenya is in East Africa and the Masai area is in southern Kenya. **Maasai** *is another spelling for this area.*

Decide with Your Student

Will you read the story aloud or will your child read it to you?
Or will you take turns reading to each other?

Introduce the Book

In this book, we will meet Linda. In school, Linda learned about Kenya in East Africa and the native people called the Masai, who live in the southern part of the country.

Linda wonders how her life would be different if she were a Masai in East Africa.

Do you ever wonder what it would be like to live in a different country?

Where would you like to go? How might life be different there for someone your age?

Read *Masai and I*

Listen and look at the pictures to see how the author and the illustrator compared and contrasted Linda's life at home and in East Africa.

How do the pictures add to the story?

After Reading

What surprised you in this story? What did you learn about the Masai culture?

What was similar and what was different about Linda's life in the United States and her life as a Masai?

Explain

This book discusses one small group of people in East Africa—the Masai. Life in big cities in Kenya is very much like Linda's life in the United States.

Homework Activity for Students
Ask your child to choose <u>ONE</u> of the following homework activities to complete and bring back to class.

a. Draw a picture of what you would like to do if you went to a Masai village.

or

b. Imagine that you live in a different country. Where might you live?_____

Draw a picture of how you imagine <u>one activity</u> in your life in that place.

or

c. If you have access to a computer, explore this website: http://pbskids.org/africa/

In the section called My World, visit one of the schools in Africa.

Write a short story (up to one page) to tell how life is different from or similar to your life for students in the school you visited.

Bolsa de Lectura (Grados 3–5)

Masai and I (Masai y Yo), escrito por Virginia Kroll
e ilustrado por Nancy Carpenter

Materiales en la Bolsa

◆ Un mapa del mundo con África, Kenia, y el área Masai en la parte sur de Kenia claramente marcado

◆ Guía para el estudiante y el padre o miembro de la familia para usar cuando se esté leyendo y conversando sobre el libro

Padres

Sugerencias de temas y preguntas para conversar con su hijo están en letra cursiva. Agregue sus propias ideas para disfrutar el libro con su hijo.

Antes de Leer

Este cuento sucede en una parte de África y es sobre un grupo de gente de esa área.

Miremos el continente de África en el mapa. Kenia se encuentra en África del Este y el área Masai está en el área sur de Kenia. **Maasai** *es otra forma de deletrear ésta área.*

Decisiones con Su Estudiante

¿Va leer el cuento en voz alta o su hijo se lo va leerá a usted?
¿O quizá tomarán turnos en leerlo uno al otro?

Presentar el Libro

En este libro, conoceremos a Linda. En su escuela, Linda aprendió sobre Kenia en África del Este y los nativos del grupo Masai, quienes viven en la parte del sur de ese país.

Linda se pregunta cómo su vida sería diferente si fuera un Masai en el África del Este.

¿Te has preguntado alguna vez cómo sería vivir en un país diferente?

¿A dónde te gustaría ir? ¿Cómo sería diferente la vida allí para una persona de tu edad?

Lee *Masai and I (Masai y Yo)*

Escucha y mira las ilustraciones para ver cómo el autor y el ilustrador compararon y contrastaron la vida de Linda en su país nativo y en África del Este.

¿Cómo le agregan las ilustraciones al cuento?

Después de Leer

¿Qué te sorprendió del cuento? ¿Qué aprendiste de la cultura Masai?

¿Qué fue parecido y diferente de la vida de Linda en los Estados Unidos y como un Masai?

Explique

Este libro habla de un pequeño grupo de gente de África del Este—los Masai. La vida en las ciudades grandes de Kenia es muy parecida a la vida de Linda en los Estados Unidos.

Actividad de Tarea para los Estudiantes
Elige UNA de las siguientes actividades. Complétala y entrégala a tu maestro.

La fecha de entrega para esta tarea es:_____.

   a. Dibuja una ilustración de lo que te gustaría hacer si fueras a un pueblo Masai.
     Escribe una o dos oraciones sobre porque escogiste esta actividad.
     Muestra tu ilustración y lee tu oración a tu padre u otro miembro de la familia.

O

   b. Imagínate que vives en un país diferente. ¿Dónde vivirías?_____
     Dibuja cómo imaginas una actividad de tu vida en ese lugar.
     Escribe una o dos oraciones sobre porque escogiste esta actividad.
     Muestra tu ilustración y lee tu oración a tu padre u otro miembro de la familia.

O

   c. Si tienes acceso a una computadora, visita el sitio http://pbskids.org/africa/
     En la sección que se llama Mi Mundo (My World), visita una de las escuelas en África.
     Escribe un cuento pequeño (máximo de una página) y explica cómo tu vida es diferente o parecida a la vida de los estudiantes en la escuela que visitaste.
     Lee tu cuento a tu padre u otro miembro de la familia.

Literacy Bag (Grades 6–8)

Sing Down the Moon, written by Scott O'Dell

Name of Student_____ Date_____

Sing Down the Moon (A Family Reading Activity)

Dear Parent/Family Partner,

We are reading historical fiction in Language Arts, including the adventures of young people from different cultures. In this assignment, I will read the story of the Navaho Indians in the 1860s and we can discuss some ideas about the book. I hope you enjoy this activity with me. This assignment and the Literacy Bag and book are due_____.

Sincerely,_____
(Student's Signature)

Procedure

1. Select a family partner (parent, grandparent, older sibling) to talk with you about this book.

   Who is your family partner?_____

2. In this story, we meet Bright Morning, a Navaho girl of fourteen. Over two years, from 1863 to 1865, she experiences major changes in her life and in her home. She becomes part of an important period of U.S. history.

3. Start at the end of the book! The postscript at the end of the book gives the history of the Navaho Indians from 1863 to 1865 on which the story is based. To share the context for this book, read the postscript aloud with your family partner <u>before</u> YOU read the story.

   a. What question do you have about the Navaho during this time period?_____

   _____

   b. What question does your family partner have about the Navaho during this time period?_____

   _____

4. Read the book during the next week. Then reflect on the story and its history with your family partner. This story touches on many important themes in the lives of Bright Morning, Tall Boy, and other characters. Check **ONE** ✓ of the following five themes that most interests you. Choose a, b, c, d, or e.

   a. ❑ **Role of family. <u>Read Chapter 20 aloud to your family partner</u>** for examples of the importance of family, tribe, and community and the role of men and women in this culture. Discuss similarities and differences in the importance of family and neighbors today.

   b. ❑ **Entering adulthood. <u>Read Chapter 13 aloud to your family partner</u>** to understand Bright Morning's experience in the Womanhood Ceremony. Discuss your reactions to this ceremony and how girls or boys enter adulthood today.

c. ❑ **Living with a physical disability. <u>Read Chapter 12 aloud to your family partner</u>** for examples of how Tall Boy, shot by the Spaniards, was affected by his injury. Discuss similarities or differences in how teens with disabilities are treated today.

d. ❑ **The Long Walk. <u>Read Chapter 17 aloud to your family partner</u>** to understand how Navaho and other Native American tribes were forced to leave their homes and relocate to enslavement camps. Discuss your reactions to the U.S. government's treatment of Native Americans at this time in history.

e. ❑ **Importance of names. <u>Read Chapter 3 aloud to your family partner</u>** to get a sense of what a person's name meant in this culture. Why do you think names were important to this tribe? What do you think your name would be if you lived at this time and why? What do you think your family member's name would be and why?

5. With your family partner, discuss why the theme you selected was important in the past for the character in the book and why it is important to you today.

Now, YOU write a paragraph or two giving your ideas on the importance of the theme—past and present. Use extra paper if you need more room.

Title: _____

_____

_____

_____

_____

_____

6. **Read your paragraph aloud to your family partner.** Fix any sentences that are unclear.

Home-to-School Communication

Dear Parent/Family Partner:

Please share your reactions to your student's work on this activity.

Write YES or NO for each statement.

_____1. My child understood the homework and was able to discuss it.

_____2. My child and I enjoyed the activity.

_____3. This assignment helped me know what my child is learning in language arts.

Other comments: _____

Signature: _____

Source: Greenfeld, M. D., Epstein, J. L., and Hutchins, D. J., *Teachers Involve Parents in Schoolwork (TIPS): Interactive Homework for the Middle Grades* (Baltimore: Center on School, Family, and Community Partnerships, Johns Hopkins University, 2012).

Lenguaje (Grados Intermedios)

Sing Down the Moon, *Escrito por Scott O'Dell*

Nombre_____ Fecha_____

Actividad De Tarea Escolar Interactiva

Estimado Padre/Miembro de la familia,

Estamos leyendo ficción histórica en la clase de Lenguaje, incluyendo las aventuras de los jóvenes de diferentes culturas. En ésta tarea, I yo voy a leer un cuento acerca de los indios Navaho en los años 1860s y me gustaría conversar sobre el libro. Espero que disfrutes ésta actividad conmigo. Esta tarea y la Bolsa de Lectura tienen fecha de entrega _____.

Sinceramente,_____
Firma del Estudiante

Procedimiento

1. Selecciona un miembro de la familia (padre, abuelo, hermano mayor) con quien hablar sobre este libro.

   ¿Quién es tu socio familiar?_____

2. En este cuento, conocimos a Mañana Brillante, una muchacha Navaho de catorce años. Durante dos años, entre 1863 y 1865, ella vive cambios mayores en su vida y en su hogar. Ella fue parte de un periodo muy importante de la historia de los Estados Unidos.

3. Anticipo: ¡Empieza al Final del Libro!

   El epílogo al final del libro presenta la historia de los Indios Navaho durante 1863 y 1865. Para compartir el contexto del libro, lee el epílogo en voz fuerte con tu miembro de la familia <u>antes</u> de leer el cuento.

   a) ¿Qué pregunta tienes acerca de los Navaho durante esa época?_____

   _____

   b) ¿Qué pregunta tiene tu miembro de la familia acerca de los Navaho durante esa época?

   _____

4. TÚ lee el libro durante la próxima semana. Reflexiona sobre el cuento y su historia con tu miembro de la familia.

   Este cuento toca muchos temas importantes de las vidas de Mañana Brillante, Niño Alto, y otros personajes. Marca **UNO** de los temas que más te interesó con un. Marca a, b, c, d, o e.

   a. ❑ **Papel de la familia. <u>Lee el capítulo 20 en voz alta a tu miembro de la familia</u>** y busca ejemplos sobre la importancia de la familia, tribu, y comunidad y el papel de los hombres y mujeres de esta cultura. Conversa de las semejanzas y diferencias en la importancia de la familia y de los vecinos hoy.

   b. ❑ **Entrando a la adultez. <u>Lee el capítulo 13 en voz alta a tu miembro de la familia</u>** para entender la experiencia de Mañana Brillante en la Ceremonia de la Femineidad. Conversa de tus reacciones sobre ésta ceremonia y cómo las niñas o niños entran a la adultez hoy.

c. ❏ **Viviendo con una incapacidad física. <u>Lee el capítulo 12 en voz alta a tu miembro de la familia</u>** y busca ejemplos sobre cómo Niño Alto, quien fue balaceado por los Españoles, fue afectado por su herida. Conversa de las semejanzas o diferencias en cómo los jóvenes incapacitados de hoy son tratados.

d. ❏ **La caminata larga. <u>Lee capítulo 17 en voz alta a tu miembro de la familia</u>** para entender cómo los Navaho y otras tribus nativas de América fueron obligados a dejar sus hogares y fueron reasignados en campamentos de esclavitud. Conversa de tus reacciones sobre el tratamiento de los nativos Americanos por el gobierno de Estados Unidos durante ese tiempo histórico.

e. ❏ **La importancia de los nombres. <u>Lee capítulo 3 en voz alta a tu miembro de la familia</u>** para obtener una idea del significado del nombre de una persona en esta cultura. ¿Por qué piensas que los nombres fueron importantes para esta tribu? ¿Cuál sería tu nombre si vivieras en ese tiempo? ¿Y por qué? ¿Cuál sería el nombre de tu miembro de la familia? ¿Y por qué?

Con tu miembro de la familia, conversa sobre la importancia en el pasado del tema que seleccionaste para el personaje del libro y por qué es importante para ti hoy.

5. Ahora, TÚ escribe uno o dos párrafos dando tus ideas sobre la importancia del tema— pasado y presente. Usa extra hojas de papel si necesitas más espacio.

Título:_____

_____

_____

_____

_____

6. **Lee tu párrafo en voz alta a tu miembro de la familia**. Arregla las oraciones que no están claras.

Comunicacion Hogar-Escuela

Estimado Padre/Miembro de la familia:

Por favor comparte sus reacciones al trabajo de su estudiante en esta actividad.

Escriba Sí o NO en cada declaración.

_____1. Mi hijo entendió la tarea y fue capaz de hablar sobre ella.

_____2. A mi hijo y a mí nos gustó mucho esta actividad.

_____3. Esta tarea me ayudó saber lo que mi hijo está aprendiendo en Lenguaje.

Otros comentarios:_____

Firma:_____

Fuente: Greenfeld, M. D., Epstein, J. L., and Hutchins, D. J., *Teachers Involve Parents in Schoolwork (TIPS): Interactive Homework for the Middle Grades* (Baltimore: Center on School, Family, and Community Partnerships, Johns Hopkins University, 2011).

Appendix

Forms for Planning Partnership Activities

Planning Committee
Planning Page

Activity: _____

Date of Activity: _____

Tasks	Person in Charge	Target Date	Notes	Completed ✓

Planning Checklist

Check only the tasks (or add others) that must be completed for this activity. In the chart, fill in the details to organize the work that must be done to ensure the success of this activity.

❑ Send home invitations to families to register for event. Collect responses.

❑ Obtain dinner donations (food, paper products, drinks, etc.).

❑ Arrange child-care providers for very young children.

❑ Obtain paper, pencils, crayons, markers, and other supplies needed.

❑ Organize and train volunteers for specific responsibilities for the event.

❑ Make copies of all handouts for the activities.

❑ Make copies of sign-in sheets and evaluation forms.

❑ Purchase or collect prizes, raffles, and other incentives, as needed.

❑ _____

❑ _____

Sign-In Sheet

Name of Activity:_____   Date/Fecha:_____

Parent's Name/ Nombre del Padre	Child's Name/ Nombre del Niño	Child's Grade Level/ Grado del Niño

Exit Evaluation
Your Ideas, Please!

_____

Title of Activity

_____

Date

Please circle the appropriate response:

I enjoyed this activity.

Strongly agree   *Agree*   *Disagree*   *Strongly disagree*

The information was useful to me.

Strongly agree   *Agree*   *Disagree*   *Strongly disagree*

Please add your comments and suggestions.

What did you enjoy most?	*How might we improve this activity?*

THANK YOU VERY MUCH FOR YOUR IDEAS!

Evaluacion de Salida
¡Sus Ideas. Por Favor!

_____
Título de la Actividad

_____
Fecha

Please circle the appropriate response:

Yo disfruté de esta actividad.

Totalmente de Acuerdo   _Acuerdo_   _Desacuerdo_   _Totalmente de Desacuerdo_

La información fue útil para mí.

Totalmente de Acuerdo   _Acuerdo_   _Desacuerdo_   _Totalmente de Desacuerdo_

Por favor, añadir sus comentarios y sugerencias.

¿Qué fue lo que más le gustó?	¿Cómo podemos mejorar esta actividad?

¡MUCHAS GRACIAS POR SUS IDEAS!

Planning Committee Activity Evaluation
To Increase the Involvement of Multicultural Families

Copy this page for each activity that is conducted and save for a cumulative record for the year.

School Name: _____ School Year: _____

Activity: _____ Date of Activity: _____

Use **Excellent (E)**, **Good (G)**, **Fair (F)**, or **Poor (P)** to rate each component of the partnership activity. Discuss whether to conduct the same or a similar activity next year and, if so, how to improve the quality of outreach to multicultural families.

Action Team Planning: How well was the activity planned? _____

Support: How helpful were ATP members and others at the school? _____

Implementation: How well was the activity implemented? _____
Did it reach the target audience? _____

Results: How well did the activity contribute to desired results? _____

Will this activity be conducted in the next school year?   _____ **YES**   _____ **NO**

If **NO**, why not? _____
_____
_____

If **YES**, what should be done to improve this activity? _____
_____
_____

Source: Adapted from "Annual Evaluation of Activities," in J. L. Epstein et al., *School, family, and community partnerships: Your handbook for action,* 3rd ed. (Thousand Oaks, CA: Corwin Press, 2009).

References

Adelman, H., & Taylor, L. (2011). *A Center policy brief: Immigrant children and youth: Enabling their success at school.* Los Angeles: School Mental Health Project at UCLA. Retrieved from http://smph.psych.ucla.edu.

Advocates for Children of New York. (2009). *Our children, our schools.* New York: Author. Retrieved from www.advocatesforchildren.org/Our_Children_Our_Schools%20_FINAL_Report.pdf.

Allen, J. (2007). *Creating welcoming schools: A practical guide to home-school partnerships with diverse families.* New York: Teachers College Press.

Arzubiaga, A. E., Nogueron, S. C., & Sullivan, A. L. (2009). The education of children in im/migrant families. *Review of Research in Education, 33,* 246–271.

Asia Society. (2010). *Ready for the world: Preparing elementary students for the global age.* New York: Author.

Banks, J., & Banks, C. A. M. (Eds.). (2004). *Handbook of research on multicultural education* (2nd ed.). San Francisco: Jossey-Bass.

Boethel, M. (2003). *Diversity: School, family, and community connections.* Austin, TX: Southwest Educational Development Laboratory.

CBS News. (2011). *Minority kids could be majority by 2023.* Retrieved from www.cbsnews.com/storeis/2009/03/05 /national/main4844040.shtml.

Chavez, C. (2007). *Five generations of a Mexican American family in Los Angeles: The Fuentes story.* Lanham, MD: Rowman and Littlefield.

Chavkin, N. (1993). *Families and schools in a pluralistic society.* Albany: SUNY Press.

Chavkin, N., & Gonzalez, D. L. (1995). *Forging partnerships between Mexican American parents and the schools. Washington, DC: Office of Educational Research and Improvement. (Eric Document Reproduction Service No. ED388489).*

Chrispeels, J. H., & Rivero, E. (2001). Engaging Latino families for student success: How parent education can reshape parents' sense of place in the education of their children. *Peabody Journal of Education, 76,* 119–169.

Dauber, S., & Epstein, J. (1993). Parents' attitudes and practices of involvement in inner city elementary and middle schools. In N. Chavkin (Ed.), *Families and schools in a pluralistic society* (pp. 53–71). Albany: SUNY Press.

Delgado-Gaitan, C. (2004). *Involving Latino families in schools.* Thousand Oaks, CA: Corwin Press.

Delgado-Gaitan, C. (2006). *Building culturally responsive classrooms: A guide for K–6 teachers.* Thousand Oaks, CA: Corwin Press.

Delgado-Gaitan, C., & Trueba, H. (1991). *Crossing cultural borders: Education for immigrant families in America.* London: Falmer.

Delpit, L. (1995). *Other people's children: Cultural conflict in the classroom.* New York: New Press.

Epstein, J. L. (1995). School/family/community partnerships: Caring for the children we share. *Phi Delta Kappan, 76,* 701–712.

Epstein, J. L. (2011). *School, family, and community partnerships: Preparing educators and improving schools* (2nd ed.). Boulder CO: Westview Press.

Epstein, J. L., & Dauber, S. (1991). School programs and teacher practices of parent involvement in inner city elementary and middle schools. *Elementary School Journal, 91,* 289–303.

Epstein, J. L., & Sheldon, S. B. (2006). Moving forward: Ideas for research on school, family, and community partnerships. In I. F. Conrad & R. Serlin (Eds.), *SAGE Handbook for research in education: Engaging ideas and enriching inquiry* (pp. 117–137). Thousand Oaks, CA: Sage.

Epstein, J. L., et al. (2009). *School, family, and community partnerships: Your handbook for action* (3rd ed.). Thousand Oaks, CA: Corwin Press.

Epstein, J. L., Galindo, C. L., & Sheldon, S. B. (2011). Levels of leadership: Effects of district and school actions on the quality of school programs of family and community involvement. *Educational Administration Quarterly*, 47, 462–495.

Epstein, J. L., & Van Voorhis, F. L. (2001). More than minutes: Teachers' roles in designing homework. *Educational Psychologist*, 36, 181–194.

Etzioni, A. (2003). *The monochrome society*. Princeton, NJ: Princeton University Press.

Fortuny, K., Hernandez, D. J., & Chaudry, A. (2010). *Young children of immigrants: The leading edge of America's future (Brief 3)*. Washington, DC: Urban Institute.

Galindo, C. L. (in press). Involving diverse families in schools. In J. A. Banks (Ed.), *Encyclopedia of Diversity in Education*. Thousand Oaks, CA: Sage.

Gay, G. (2000). *Culturally responsive teaching: Theory, research, and practice*. New York: Teachers College Press.

Gong, G. (2008). *From ironing board to corporate board: My Chinese laundry experience in America*. Paramus, NJ: Homa & Secky Books.

Gonzalez, N., Moll, L. C., & Amanti, C. (Eds.). (2005). *Funds of knowledge: Theorizing practices in households, communities, and classrooms*. Mahwah, NJ: Erlbaum.

Hall, E. (1976). *Beyond culture*. New York: Anchor Books. (See variations on the cultural iceberg diagram at www.culturaliceberg.com/htm.)

Han, Y-C. (2010). *Lessons learned from immigrant families*. Retrieved from www.colorincolorado.org/article/38575?theme=print.

Henderson, A. T., Mapp, K. L., Johnson, V. R., & Davies, D. (2007). *Beyond the bake sale: The essential guide to family-school partnerships*. New York: New Press.

Hutchins, D. J., et al. (2010). *Promising partnership practices 2010*. Baltimore: National Network of Partnership Schools at Johns Hopkins University.

Hutchins, D. J., et al. (2011). *Promising partnership practices 2011*. Baltimore: National Network of Partnership Schools at Johns Hopkins University.

Jordan, D. (2002). *Parent and professional collaboration: A cultural perspective* (CD). Minneapolis, MN: Pacer Center.

Kugler, E. G. (2012). *Innovative voices in education: Engaging diverse communities*. Lanham, MD: Rowman and Littlefield.

Ladson-Billings, G. (1995). But that's just good teaching! The case for culturally relevant pedagogy. *Theory into Practice*, 34, 159–165.

Ladson-Billings, G. (2004). New directions in multicultural education: Complexities, boundaries, and critical race theory. In J. A. Banks & C. M. Banks (Eds.), *Handbook of research on multicultural education* (2nd ed.) (pp. 50–65). San Francisco: Jossey-Bass.

Mancilla-Martinez, J., & Kieffer, M. J. (2010). Language minority learners' home language use is dynamic. *Educational Researcher*, 39, 545–546.

Marsh, M. M., & Turner-Vorbeck, T. (2009). *(Mis)understanding families: Learning from real families in our schools*. New York: Teachers College Press.

MetLife, Inc. (2010). *The MetLife survey of the American teacher: Preparing students for college and careers. Part 2: Teaching diverse learners.* New York: Author.

Moll, L. C., Amanti, C., Neff, D., & Gonzalez, N. (1992). Funds of knowledge for teaching: Using a qualitative approach to connect homes and classrooms. *Theory into Practice, 31,* 132–141.

Moll, L., & Ruiz, R. (2002). The schooling of Latino children. In M. Suárez-Orozco & M. Páez (Eds.), *Latinos remaking America* (pp. 362–375). Berkeley: University of California Press.

National Center for Education Statistics. (2009). *Schools and staffing survey.* Table 3: Percentage distribution of students, by sex, race/ethnicity, school type, and selected school characteristics 2007–09. Retrieved from http://neces.ed.gov/pubs2009/2009321/tables/sass0708_20093321_212n_03 asp.

National Network of Partnership Schools (NNPS). (2011). *Promising Partnership Practices.* http://www.csos. jhu.edu/p2000/success.htm

Nieto, S., & Bode, P. (2011). *Affirming diversity: The sociopolitical context of multicultural education* (6th ed.). Boston, MA: Allyn & Bacon.

Northeast and Islands Regional Educational Laboratory at Brown University (LAB). (2002). *The diversity kit: An introductory resource for social change in education.* Providence, RI: Brown University. www.alliance. brown.edu/tdl/diversitykit.shtml.

Reardon, S. F., & Galindo, C. (2009). The Hispanic-White achievement gap in math and reading in the elementary grades. *American Educational Research Journal, 46,* 853–891.

Richardson, T. (2011). At the garden gate: Community building through food—revisiting the critique of "food, folk, and fun" in multicultural education. *Urban Review, 43,* 107–123.

Rodriguez-Brown, F. V. (2009). *The home-school connection: Lessons learned in a culturally and linguistically diverse community.* New York: Routledge.

Saint Paul Public Schools. (2010). http://datacenter.spps.org/.

Salinas, K. C., & Jansorn, N. R. (2003). *Promising partnership practices 2003.* Baltimore: National Network of Partnership Schools at Johns Hopkins University.

Sanders, M. G. (2006). *Building school-community partnerships: Collaboration for student success.* Thousand Oaks, CA: Corwin Press.

Sheldon, S. B. (2009). Improving student outcomes with school, family, and community partnerships: A research review. In J. Epstein et al., *School, family, and community partnerships: Your handbook for action* (3rd ed.) (pp. 40–56). Thousand Oaks, CA: Corwin Press.

Sleeter, C. M., & Grant, C. (2003). *Making choices for multicultural education: Five approaches to race, class, and gender* (4th ed). Danvers, MA: Wiley.

Stepanek, J., & Raphael, J. (2010). Creating schools that support success for English language learners. *Education Northwest Lessons Learned, 1*(2), 1–4 (September).

Suárez-Orozco, C., & Suárez-Orozco, M. (2001). *Children of immigration.* Cambridge, MA: Harvard University Press.

Suárez-Orozco, C., Rhodes, J., & Milburn, M. (2009). Unraveling the immigrant paradox: Academic engagement and disengagement among recently arrived immigrant youth. *Youth and Society, 41,* 151–185.

Valdes, G. (1996). *Con respeto: Bridging distances between culturally diverse families and schools.* New York: Teachers College Press.

Waterman, R., & Harry, B. (2008). *Building collaboration between schools and parents of English Language Learners: Transcending barriers, creating opportunities.* Tempe, AZ: National Center for Culturally Responsive Educational Systems.

Weiss, H. B., Lopez, M. E., & Rosenberg, H. (2010). *Beyond random acts: Family, school, and community engagement as an integral part of education reform.* Washington, DC: National Policy Forum for Family, School, & Community Engagement.

Wilkerson, I. (2010). *The warmth of other suns: The epic story of America's great migration.* New York: Random House.

Woyshner, C. (2009). *The National PTA, race, and civic engagement, 1897–1970.* Columbus: Ohio State University Press.

Zehr, M. A. (2009). English learners pose policy puzzle. *Education Week Quality Counts*, 28 (17), 8–9 (January 8, 2009).